About the Author

Santosh Nair is the Chairman and Chief Mentor of **smm**art Training & Consultancy Services Pvt. Ltd, one of India's finest entrepreneurial transformation companies. An ace trainer, motivational speaker and coach, his expertise lies in sales, leadership, and entrepreneurship. He brings a lethal combination of life-transforming philosophies with contemporary examples in his larger than life, powerful style of delivery, which makes him the most preferred trainer across masses and classes.

Santosh's intense training programmes and high energy speeches have led to the skill and productivity enhancement of some of the finest national and international corporations such as Vodafone, Asian Paints, Proctor & Gamble, HDFC, ICICI, Coca Cola, Airtel, Blowplast, ITW India, Sodexo Pass, Mahindra & Mahindra, Saint Gobain Glass, Philips, Ion Exchange, Godrej, LIC, Tata Motors, Motilal Oswal Securities Ltd., New Holland Tractor, Hyundai Motors, etc.

Having transformed the lives of over 2 million people and more than 1500 real-time entrepreneurs, Nair has dedicated his life to the cause of entrepreneurial excellence and acts as an entrepreneurial coach helping small- and medium-sized entrepreneurs envision and reach a greater future. He has to his credit over a hundred life transforming audios and videos on generic subjects — each aimed at awakening human talent to their present realities and unleashing their true potential. His mission in life is to inspire at least one human being every day.

Praise for the Book

The best part of this book is that you can read it from start to end in one go... it's truly inspirational!

— Radhakrishnan Pillai
Author – Corporate Chanakya
Director – Chanakya Institute of Public leadership, University of Mumbai

Santosh's personal stories of struggles, failures, perseverance and triumphs differentiate this book from everything that's out there on self-help and leadership. Go read!

— Akhshay Gaonkar
National Head – Prepaid Acquisitions
Corporate Product Marketing
Idea Cellular

For Santosh, enthusiasm and next level vision is his passion that is reflected in this book. The book inspires 'creative restlessness' and 'positive dissatisfaction' to achieve an entrepreneurial drive.

— B. O. Mehta
Sr. President
Pidilite Industries Ltd.

Hard hitting, strong, and compelling. Keeps your interest alive and forces you to go into deep reflection to discover who you are and where you want to reach. Well written like a story with practical exercises after each chapter helping readers convert concepts to practical use, making this book unique.

— Rajendra Sud
Director & Head — New Initiatives
Max Life Insurance Co. Ltd.

This book was really enjoyable. A 'must read' for all budding entrepreneurs...

— Mahesh Shetty
CMD
MT Educare Ltd
(The man behind Mahesh Tutorials)

Santosh's straight-from-the-heart, high-energy, passionate messages conveyed in this book motivate and engage all readers, providing them with the eleven commandments that are the guiding principles to live an extraordinary life!

— Warren Patrick
Senior Vice President & Group Head of Learning
Edelweiss Capital
Former Sr. Vice President – Training & Development, HSBC Bank

This book contains many maxims which speak about how a 'progressive mindset' should be! It's a prescription for lifetime growth and living a meaningful life, something that Santosh practises himself. A must read for all those who want to become 'relevant' and 'stay relevant'.

— Anil Jha
Sr. Business Associate
Life Insurance Corporation of India
(India's leading Development Officer)

Santosh has transferred his enthusiasm to the reader through this book. This book will inspire you to action, bring about an incredible transformation in your personality, unleash your creative but hidden energy, and guide you towards the crest of excellence.

— Bharat Parekh

India's No.1 Life Insurance Agent

18 times MDRT Qualifier (Million Dollar Round Table)

12 times COT Qualifier (Court of the Table)

8 times TOT Qualifier (Top of the Table)

Santosh Nair's entrepreneurial spirit and uncanny ability to inspire people and facilitate the maximization of their potential was amply evident from his early years. That he has been able to blossom from a budding motivator of a few to one of the premier motivators of many, is for me a matter of personal delight. I am sure that this book which crystallizes his life's philosophy will be a powerful catalyst of change for all those who read it.

— Cynthia D'Souza

Managing Director

Cynthesis Management Consultants Pvt. Ltd.

Former Head of HR & Learning – Coca Cola, India

Former Group Director, HR – Parke-Davis Warner-Lambert

Anyone who wants to learn how to swim against the tide and live an extraordinary life by creating history rather than reading it or becoming history, *Eleven Commandments of Life Maximization* is the book for you!

— Rajesh Agnelo Athaide

CMD

St. Angelos Professional Education

A difficult subject explained in an inspiring way, this book is for those who are not happy with status quo, and by implication, it is for everybody!

— Vivek S. Patwardhan
Executive Coach & OD Consultant
Former Vice President, HR – Asian Paints

This book captures the quintessential 'Santosh Nair' — a passionate teacher who learns, practises best practices and further enhances them through reflection and repetition. The book is an easy read and a great addition to the self-improvement genre.

— Uma Devaguptapu
Corporate Director – HR
India MEA SE Asia, Illinois Tool Works (ITW India Ltd.)

Eleven Commandments of Life Maximization is an inspiring, provocative, action-oriented piece of excellence written in a passionate and forceful manner to evoke nothing less than self-maximization as a result.

— L. Jaipal Reddy
Ex. M.D. of V.I.P. Undergarments & Director of Lovable Lingerie

Espousing the tenets elucidated in this book will help you delve into the deep recesses of your inner being and unleash the unfathomable power within you to make you a leader for life!

— Samson Sequeira
International Ultra Marathoner
Marathon & Fitness Trainer

The wisdom contained within the pages of *Eleven Commandments of Life Maximization* comprises the kind of practical learning most individuals are unable to master despite a lifetime of practice. Santosh Nair has produced a brilliant guide for Life Maximization... a must read and more importantly, a must do.

— A. W. George
Managing Director
TPCL, India
Former Business Head, Hero Mindmine
[HERO Group]

This book, in a nutshell, gives you life's success formulas, which if internalized would definitely make you a 'Meaningful Specific' rather than a 'Wandering Generality'.

— Nayan Kamat
Associate Vice President - Sales
Vodafone

"Real life experiences of one of the smartest and most successful salesmen and trainers –Santosh Nair – captured in this book will surely inspire many young and aspiring Indians."

— Aporesh Acharya
Director of Training, MILT Training Foundation (India)
Former Trainer of Dale Carnegie Associates, USA

"This book creates a sense of restlessness and agitation in a progressive soul. Truly transformational… will give birth to a refined human being within you."

— R.K. Shetty
Chairman - 2013 MDRT Experience Task Force
Top of The Table (USA)

"From the very beginning to the end the reader is kept interested using the numerous citations from the lives of famous personalities as well as his personal life. Unlike other books of a philosophical nature, this book did not bore me even for a second. Each commandment has been explained in such a way that every individual can picture how his life will change if he abides by the rules of the book.

One of the most likable parts of the book was the blank space given to the reader to immediately fill in the thoughts that first come to his mind while reading a particular part of the book. Due to this, after a point, the book begins to interact with the reader, becoming his personal psychologist."

— **Manan Mehta**

Student of Bachelor in Business Administration

Praise for the Author

Empowering people to realize that they determine the outcome of their destiny is always a daunting task and only those who have tread the path, can effectively rise to this formidable endeavour. At the outset, it was obvious that Santosh truly believed that only he could determine his destiny. His innate ability to convert every challenge into an opportunity, maximize every resource around him, as well as go beyond the expected and deliver the unexpected, made it inevitable that he would emerge a winner.

Always a possibility thinker and one to never take 'no' for an answer, Santosh was never afraid to rock the boat in the middle of the sea which is precisely what he did, when he unlocked the key to maximizing his own life and achieve great success. He set out on his own to show others how they could transform their lives too. Drawing from his rich and vast life experience, he created a road map for maximizing potential, enriching the quality of life and making it productive and fulfilling. Combining it with his inherent gift of being able to influence people and sell impossible ideas, he has been able to impact the lives of many young people and inspire them to follow in his footsteps.

This delightful book, which encapsulates the life maximization philosophy that Santosh embraces, urges people to raise their standards, challenge their limiting beliefs, and engage in transformational change. If enough people read this book and sincerely apply its commandments, it would certainly change the complexion of their future and that of the world around them. In doing so, he would indeed have realized his dream of being a 'leader for life'.

— **Suresh** L. **Goklaney**
Executive Vice Chairman, Eureka Forbes Ltd.

Walking the talk! Santosh Nair is one man who has done it, and millions have followed.

At the age of 27, having become the CEO of one of the largest companies in the world, with IIM (Ahmedabad) and engineering degrees under my belt, I thought I was the king of the world. And then I met Santosh. I began to understand how much more I had to learn — about business, people, management, leadership, about life, and about myself.

He again inspired me when I was leading a 10,000-strong team and motivated me to rock my boat, giving birth to the entrepreneur inside me. Over the years, Santosh became my guiding light, leading me to success.

The Eleven Commandments mentioned in this book are really the gospel truths he has practised through his life. I have tried to follow them too, resulting in clarified vision, unbridled energy, and incredible results.

If there is one book that you must not only read, but also adopt as your life's mantra, this is it.

— Ravi Saxena
CEO of MISB Bocconi School of Business
MD of Wonderchef Home Appliances
Former Managing Director – Sodexo

(Now a successful entrepreneur, Ravi is credited with building companies and brands like Sodexo, Gloria Jeans Coffees, Fun City and The Yellow Chilli Restaurants employing over 75,000 people in India.)

Having created and nurtured a business for the last 17 years, most of my insights about playing the game of life have come from the University of Hard Knocks.

I learnt early in my career that the worst kind of fool keeps repeating old mistakes. The smart ones learn and move on. The smartest ones not only gather insights from their own lives but also embrace strategies devised by wise ones like Santosh Nair!

I consider Santosh a fellow-traveller and a twin-soul in this journey called life. Many of the precious insights he shares so generously in this book, mirror my own observations on the subject of success. Santosh articulates philosophies, ethics, attitudes and strategies that have not found their way into self-help literature so far. These insights have nevertheless profited several tough-nosed businessmen I know who have intuitively arrived at the same conclusions.

Eleven Commandments of Life Maximization is a blockbuster of a book from a man who has a passion for taking life by the lapels and succeeding against all odds. I recommend this book to all entrepreneurs, marketers, and professionals who wish to make a success of their lives and businesses.

— **Sanjeev Gupta**
Managing Director
Global Advertisers

Santosh Nair is a high-calibre professional and has been a top performer in all his roles. He is a lot of fun to work with as he has an infectious enthusiasm combined with deep diligence and a penchant for detailed application.

His positive 'can do' attitude towards work and life, influences friends and colleagues equally. He not only believes in performance and delivery, but also in grooming all those who work with him.

I wish him the very best.

— A. W. George
Managing Director
TPCL, India
Former Business Head, Hero Mindmine
[HERO Group]

ELEVEN COMMANDMENTS *of* LIFE MAXIMIZATION

Be a Leader for Life

SANTOSH NAIR

JAICO PUBLISHING HOUSE

Ahmedabad Bangalore Chennai
Delhi Hyderabad Kolkata Mumbai

Published by Jaico Publishing House
A-2 Jash Chambers, 7-A Sir Phirozshah Mehta Road
Fort, Mumbai - 400 001
jaicopub@jaicobooks.com
www.jaicobooks.com

ELEVEN COMMANDMENTS OF LIFE MAXIMIZATION
ISBN 978-81-8495-378-7

First Jaico Impression: 2013
12th Jaico Impression: 2024

Page design and layouts: Special Effects, Mumbai

Printed by
Trinity Academy For Corporate Training Limited, Mumbai

Contents

Acknowledgements

Writing a book was always on my agenda, but I didn't know it would happen so soon. And then came the tenth of February 2011, when I conducted my public seminar 'Eleven Commandments of Life Maximization' for over 2500 people, in an auditorium in Mumbai. It was there that the first seed of writing this book was sown by the Chief Editor of Jaico Publications—Mr. Rayasam Sharma, whom I now fondly call Sharmaji.

This book would not have been possible without the initiative of Sharmaji who urged me to write this book and the little young angel Poornima who vehemently pursued it and because of her diligent follow-ups and reminders ensured that I completed my task within the timeframe. For as long as I continue to exist on this planet, my birth and emergence as an author will be accredited to the tireless efforts of Jaico Publications.

Dedications

- This book is dedicated to my father, Mr. K. S. Nair, for I learned to be tough from him.
- To my mother, Indira S Nair, for her passion and craze to never see me down.
- To my sisters Sudha Nair & Seema Menon, whose belief in me strengthened my belief in myself.
- To my wife Sindhu, whose extraordinary, unconditional love helped me unleash my true potential.
- To my three beautiful daughters, Devika, Malavika & Radhika, who did not demand my time when I was on the go.
- To my numerous bosses and super bosses —

  Anil Kumar Gupta, Anil Ambo Liloo Batra, Rajesh Malhotra, Vinod Swami, Cynthia D'Souza, Suresh Goklaney, Akhil Marfatia, A. K. Subramaniam, P. K. Roy, A. V. Suresh, Manish Kaul, Ashok Kumar,
- Arun Nalvade, John Selveraj, J. P. Singh and A. W. George, whose wisdom made me what I am today.

- → To all my present & past colleagues, subordinates and staff at smmart, whose unconditional surrender helped maximize my life to the fullest.
- → To my innumerable customers, clients and well wishers all over the world, whose boundless support and love shaped me into a great salesman, sales manager, leader, trainer, coach and entrepreneur.
- → To the great thinkers and philosophers, whose life, methods, books, audios, videos, and entire existence told me that they were not the benchmark that I should look up to, but only milestones from where I was expected to start.
- → And lastly, to Nausheen Merchant, my Executive Assistant, whose abilities and willingness I have never been in a position to fathom. Without her, this book could not have seen the light of the day. Thank you Nausheen, for your unconditional surrender that helped bring out the best in me. Thank you for writing this book with me... thank you for converting my thoughts into words.

Foreword

In today's dynamic and fast-paced world, it is becoming increasingly challenging to sustain the energy and enthusiasm of the human spirit. For one to live a gratifying life amidst arduous physical and mental demands, would mean maximizing talent, capabilities, and maximizing life as a whole. This ability to maximize does not happen accidentally, unknowingly, or reactively. Maximization is a very deliberate and conscious effort.

I have known Santosh for over a decade now, and have always admired his enthusiasm, energy, and passion to take life head on. Santosh has only grown in his intensity, impact, and enthusiasm. His journey with my organisation Mahindra & Mahindra began in 1998 and since then I have seen him inspire many of my colleagues across the Group's companies.

The book *Eleven Commandments of Life Maximization* is a very candid and lucid articulation of his zeal and enthusiasm for life. In this book, Santosh challenges every aspect of life and demonstrates how he has demanded excellence from himself, disregarded difficulties, defied accepted norms of society, said no to conventional thinking and always remained a W.I.P.

(Work In Progress). He also reveals how one can consciously maximize life by following eleven simple commandments to live an extraordinary life, not just for oneself, but also to transform others around them.

Maximizing one's life means unleashing your true potential, optimizing the world around you and realizing that your existence creates a multiplier effect. In order to maximize your potential, you need to be self-constituted, in a state of liberation and confidence, and not be governed by external forces. By utilizing every available resource, drawing from the energy and charisma of others, learning and studying them; by remaining focused on your own goals and ambitions regardless of life's unpredictable circumstances; by consciously defocusing ourselves from the various emotion draining distractions surrounding us, we will be able to produce maximum results and realize our full potential.

Santosh has also emphasized the importance of doing things differently, challenging the status quo and experimenting when there is no obvious need to do so. Having reached the peak of one's business/career, when everything is going well, life is steady and productivity is at its best, it is a great challenge to experiment, innovate, and create ripples. A belief that the future is an extension of the past restricts greater possibilities.

Therefore, for one to maximize life, one should have a burning desire to constantly Rise and enable others to Rise. Once these thoughts and words become our actions, our possibilities are endless. The philosophy of Rise that drives the Mahindra Group has enabled us to evolve solutions that power mobility, drive rural prosperity, and enhance lifestyles. This essence of Rise resonates with Santosh's philosophy and you will see references to it several times in the book.

This book, therefore, is a fitting tribute to the human spirit and a good read for everyone who wishes to maximize their life.

— Dr. Pawan Goenka

President

Automotive and Farm Equipment Sectors

Mahindra & Mahindra Ltd.

Preface

I have delivered over a hundred programmes so far on diverse subjects, but 'Eleven Commandments of Life Maximization' is by far my uncontested best — the one which is the closest to my heart for the simple reason that this programme carries the entire essence of my life and the finest, the most fundamental and life changing lessons and experiences learnt over the past 29 years of being a salesman, a sales manager, sales leader, a trainer, consultant, coach, mentor, enabler, and rising up the ranks to being one of India's best known and well-regarded Sales, Confidence and Motivational Gurus, an Entrepreneurial Coach, and an Entrepreneur myself. This book is the manuscript of this very invaluable programme.

I hope that the contents of this book help you maximize your life as much as they have helped me.

Warning

This book is only for those who want to live, learn, love, and leave a legacy behind.

This is not for the ordinary mortals and faint-hearted, but for all those who are normal and have the guts to become abnormal, and are willing to pay the price for what that abnormality brings.

Life Maximization — An Introduction

Life has to be maximized; else your visit to this planet has been a waste.

There are two types of people I have met in my life — the first category of people come and go from this world with no significant difference made by their existence. Except for their close family members, friends, and colleagues nobody ever knows of that person's existence. He or she is an ordinary son or daughter, an ordinary husband or wife, an ordinary father or mother, an ordinary entrepreneur with an ordinary life, ordinary thoughts, and ordinary ways of living life. Their view about themselves, their life and future are all ordinary and with this ordinary self, he or she lives within a comfort zone, having very little or no influence even on his or her immediate companions/surroundings. I call these human beings, in the words of Zig Ziglar, the 'Wandering Generality' and their life is spent wandering as part of the larger crowd.

The second category of people is the exact opposite of the first. They leave a lasting impact on the world around them. They are the ones who rise above the crowd and make it big in life by the huge contributions that they make to their industries, society, and humanity at large. Take for instance the legacy of A.R. Rahman, Baba Amte (the man who built a home for leprosy patients), Martin Luther King, Steve Jobs (of Apple Inc.), Nelson Mandela, and others.

They are known for their meaningful lives, for the sacrifices, pain, and trauma they have undergone, for the bold decisions they took; the challenges, and long, unending opposition they have faced, and the spirit, tenacity, passion, and obsession that they possessed through their life, not allowing any negative circumstance to crack them. How else can you define the life of Nelson Mandela who continued with his fight for the rights of the black people even after 26 years of imprisonment — a considerable amount of time that can drain a human being of the will to even live life, let alone fight for a cause.

These people belong to the second category known as the 'Meaningful Specific'. People who have a long and sustained track record for living an extraordinary life — who have consistently lived the life of a role model — whose thoughts, words, deeds, and actions are leading examples that ordinary people look up to and emulate. Their presence becomes an occasion to celebrate and their absence creates a vacuum, an emptiness that cannot be filled by another person over an entire lifetime.

Life changes for those around them for as long as they exist and even after that. They are the ones who become the reason for several others to exist; they are the ones who live a life bigger than themselves — a life that cannot be duplicated.

Millions and billions of people come into this world, spend their life, and go away, but there are very few who *live life* before they pass on.

Living life and spending life are two opposite ideas:

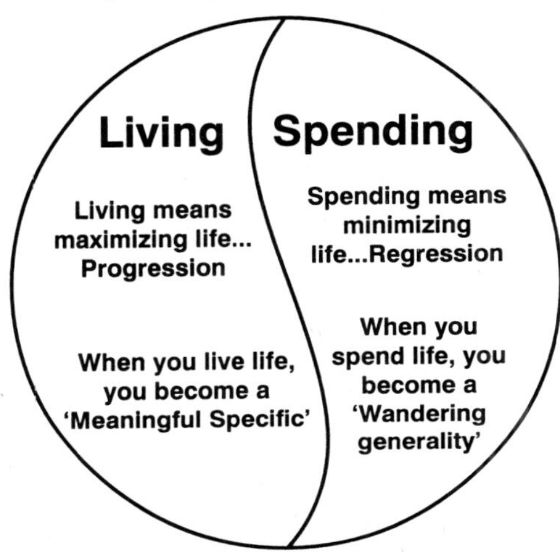

Very few people belong to the category of Meaningful Specific people (5%) whereas the rest of the population resides in the world of the Wandering Generality. The Wandering Generality are hereby referred as the 'Ordinary Mortals' and the Meaningful Specific as 'Life Maximizers.'

When we were kids, we all aspired to become Amitabh Bachchan, Neil Armstrong, Bill Gates (Microsoft), i.e. be part of the Meaningful Specific group, but as we grew older, the difficulties and complexities of the present became too overwhelming to allow us to pursue our purpose in life and we ended up forming a part of the Wandering Generality.

So how do you rise above this category and place yourself in the illustrious group? What is it that makes that 5% the Meaningful Specific and distinguishes them from the crowd?

Well, I chose to be a Meaningful Specific on 4 October, 1985, the day I joined Eureka Forbes as a salesman and since then I have been consistently maximizing life for the past 29 years. In this process, I realised one thing.

Those who decide…

Those who decide to be one of the Meaningful Specific…

Consciously or unconsciously follow the art of 'Life Maximization'.

What is Life Maximization?

Life is a gift from God and all of us have been blessed with this magnanimous gift maybe 20, 30, 40, 50, or 60 years ago. Most people go to their grave using only 5% of their potential and the remaining 95% of their real capacity, capability, passion, energy, and the real purpose of their lives remains unexplored. They die with the music inside them unsung, the notes unplayed. The only way to justify this gift and make the most of life is to maximize it to the fullest and the process of doing so is called 'Life Maximization'.

People like Narayan Murthy (Infosys), Sardar Vallabhbhai Patel, Ela Bhatt (the lady behind the grand movement of SEWA — the Self Employed Women's Association), Aamir Khan, Peter Drucker, John D. Rockefeller, Benjamin Franklin, Winston Churchill, Thomas Jefferson, George Washington, Walt Disney (Disneyland), Albert Einstein, John. F. Kennedy, Helen Keller, Henry Ford (Ford Motors), Sam Walton (Walmart), Ray Kroc (McDonalds) and others like them are examples of those who optimally maximized their life by exploring their fullest potential. They are ageless, timeless, ceaseless individuals and that is what makes them part of the Meaningful Specific.

The thoughts behind Life Maximization and the philosophies driving this thought process will become clearer as we advance towards its definition that I have put together by condensing the essence of my vast and diverse experience through the last 29 years of training over 200-odd transnational corporations. This training has helped transform the lives of over 12.5 lakh individuals, hundreds and thousands of micro-mini-small and medium entrepreneurs and running smmart for the past 12 years.

This definition is extremely difficult and intense, but an important extract of life, which needs to be drilled into your psyche to let the magic of Life Maximization happen to you. I would therefore suggest that this be put up in your house — in the bathroom, by the bedside, on the refrigerator, next to the television, around your study, if not tattooed on your body to become the most unforgettable part of your life.

And here is that million dollar definition:

Life Maximization is a long, lonely process of continuously expiring your current self, thinking beyond possibilities and distancing yourself from emotionally draining distractions by single-handedly maximizing all resources around you and rocking the boat of life in the middle of the sea such that you live a life which is autonomous, forever alive, led by strong thoughts, words and deeds, that of a leader and difficult to be duplicated, thereby maximizing life for a lifetime.

No! Your professional intelligence and calibre is not at stake if you have not been able to grasp the above extract in the first go. As I said, this is a difficult and intense statement, which is bound to mystify you the first time you read it. But as you read it a number of times, you will see a reflection of this definition in the lives of all the great men and women I referred to earlier.

And when I looked at the lives of these legendary icons on the day that I started my journey of Life Maximization in 1985, I realised there is something structurally different and unusual about them. There was something in the affairs of this breed of people that told me that:

They were wired differently.

They were instructed.

And now, when I started writing this book, I realised that:

They were instructed internally.

I call these instructions, 'Commandments' that will guide you through this path of Life Maximization.

Wait… did I just say *Commandments*? But aren't the Commandments the rules set forth by God? And if yes, how will these rules help in the process of Life Maximization?

Well, it's true that the word 'Commandment' instantly strikes a chord with those who know the Ten Commandments that were given to Moses directly by Him, and instructed the Hebrews about how to live their life on earth. But does the word 'Commandment' only denote a religiously permissible way of living, or can it be looked at from outside the boundaries of religion as well?

What are Commandments?

A commandment, as defined by the *Oxford Dictionary* means:

- ➜ A Law of God
- ➜ Mandate
- ➜ An instruction
- ➜ Directive
- ➜ Order

…given to guide behaviour or action towards righteous conduct, which need not necessarily be religious in nature.

Over the past, I have accumulated eleven instructions, orders, mandates, and directives that I gave myself many, many years ago and these instructions, orders, mandates, and directives have led to my systematic, continuous, and progressive growth as a human being through the past 29 years, for I allowed the God within me to direct me throughout this journey and I directed the thoughts, words, and deeds of Santosh Nair.

I had given him a mandate; instructed him to do certain things; ordered him to lead life in a particular manner; and demanded out of him a pattern. Yes! He was instructed from within and I gave him that instruction.

I don't know if you have given yourself a Commandment; I don't know if you will ever give yourself one, but if you ever decide to, today is the day, the perfect day to give yourself the commandments to live, love, learn, and leave behind a legacy... provided you want to be a Meaningful Specific, provided you are in the game of Life Maximization!

As I write this book, I present to you the 'Eleven Commandments of Life Maximization' that you need to give yourself to commence the journey of maximizing life. It is a revelation that will transform the very meaning and perspective of your life and if taken seriously and followed religiously will take you to unbelievable heights.

As we move towards the Commandments, let me warn you that this path is very painful, laborious, challenging, and larger than life. My only request is to be with me as I unveil each of these Commandments with my own experiences, successes, and tragedies.

In the same breath, let me also tell you that this is no ordinary book, my friends. Nothing like the hundreds that you would have read in the past. Here, we are talking about Life Maximization, i.e. living a life that would have otherwise taken 40 lifetimes to be duplicated. This cannot be a book that you read to pass some time during a journey, or while resting in your armchair, or as a source of motivation just before you retire for the day. This is a way more serious affair than that!

Trying to understand and imbibe the wisdom I have garnered over the past 29 years in just one reading would be an act of utter foolishness. In order for you to allow the true magic of this book to happen to you and the real essence to sink into your psyche, it is important that you fully internalize this subject and the only way to do this is to dedicate adequate time and attention to interpreting each word mentioned here, before moving to the next one.

I would therefore request you to not read this book in one sitting. Read it chapter by chapter; mull over it for a while; ponder over it; deliberate it; write down a promise that only after reading every chapter, and reading every Commandment a minimum of three times, WILL YOU PROCEED TO THE NEXT ONE.

Dedicate a 200-page notebook to this manuscript and call it your 'Life Maximization Handbook'. Within 24 hours of reading a chapter, write down every thing that you learn in that book. Every chapter suggests some actionables; execute the action plan only after you have read each chapter thrice and written down what you understood in the Handbook.

I welcome you to Santosh Nair's world as you begin your journey of Life Maximization.

1

Declare your expiry date

Always remain a Work in Progress (WIP), else your ego will take over, making you feel you have arrived. This is where growth stops.

One may wonder what the 'expiry date' is, in the context of life maximization. Just like the 'best before' date for medicine, is the expiry date the day till when you will live on this planet, or the date up to when one may decide to continue working? That is not what I mean by the expiry date.

Currently, you may be working in a certain manner, managing teams in a certain way, interviewing people in a certain style, dealing with your children/spouse/bosses/colleagues in a peculiar fashion, working in a particular market, operating under a specific business model. Everything you are practising right now has already become a pattern for you and given the returns that it could. If you continue pursuing the same pattern, it will not yield any better results. In fact, you will not even get the desired results anymore as the current pattern has lost its relevance.

The expiry date refers to a date on which you will expire your current self and everything that you are currently doing, to rise to the next level.

What happens when you consume a medicine after its date of expiry — it either gives you a negative reaction/side effect or it does not have any effect at all. Similarly, after a point of time, if you continue using the same expired methods of walking, talking, working, behaving, dressing up, presenting yourself, they will have the same effect as expired medicine — either they will be futile and stop producing the desired results, or they may even backfire and lead to a more detrimental outcome, worsening the situation even more and with this, you will never be able to change the nature of things around you, upgrade or maximize your life.

Therefore, you need to constantly ask yourself, 'Have I become the paracetamol that does not control temperature anymore? Am

I the antibiotic that does not cure an ailment? Have I become the guitar that does not produce the required chords? Have I become a stale rose that does not spread fragrance anymore?' If you get an answer in the affirmative, you know it is time for you to rise up to the next level. And, whenever you want to rise in life, you need to declare that date as your expiry date.

Extinguish yourself periodically and rise. Emerge as someone new, different, and better.

The most apparent and living example of someone who is constantly expiring his current self and rising to the next level is the great Bollywood actor Aamir Khan who is regarded as the king of innovation and creativity in the Indian film industry. Starting with his chocolate boy image in *Qayamat Se Qayamat Tak* to the cool dude in *Dil Chahta Hai,* the rural rebel against the unjust tax practices in *Lagaan,* the mature special education school teacher in *Taare Zameen Par,* the bindaas and radical collegian in *3 Idiots,* the aggressive lead in *Ghajini* and the daring talk show host in the recent television revolution *Satyamev Jayate,* he continues to surprise his audience each time by bringing in newer and newer flavours in his next appearance and so is considered as an actor par excellence.

To walk on the path of life maximization, this expiration of your current self and renewal from time to time is essential, necessary, and mandatory.

D & D — Decision and Declaration

Let alone deciding to expire your current self, it is equally important, or rather more important, to declare this date. One may quickly take the decision to expire one's current self, but be very reluctant to declare this publically. Life Maximization happens only when you make a public declaration.

But, you may ask, why declare this? This leads us to explore the theory of:

PP v/s PP — Private Pressure v/s Public Pressure

When you declare to the world that your current self will expire and your current way of getting things done will be transformed so you rise up to the next level — you have no option, but to do it. You cannot escape from the commitment, since you have publically declared your intention. And if you do not act on it, people will ridicule you. Public pressure builds up and you are forced to transform.

For instance, if you decide that by a particular day you will move from speaking only in Marathi to speaking in English, but you do not declare this to the world, you will allow issues (this could be an urgent work assignment, a sudden debacle at the plant, or a family tragedy) that are bound to crop up before the day you start your new action, distracting you from your decision and pushing it to the backseat. There is no moral pressure on you to act on your declaration; you always have the option of not adhering to that date; after all, you are not answerable to anyone!

Now let us imagine you have decided to move from speaking only in Marathi to speaking in English by a particular day and you declare this to the world. However grave the crisis you may have to face in the meanwhile, you will still have to honour your commitment, since you are now answerable to several people if you don't. You will be questioned and ridiculed for not adhering to what you have promised. This external pressure ensures that you do what you had decided to and thereby rise to the next level.

All those who lived, loved, learned, and left a legacy are public figures and they could live, love, learn and leave a legacy only because they chose to go public about their intentions.

And yet, many people do not declare their decisions to the world because the public pressure is too painful to bear and impossible to sustain and in the process they are unable to reach their destination.

Once you announce your plans, you will, will, will, and will expire your current self — you have no alternative.

Make a list of all the things that you want to expire. Jot down the deadline and the methodology you will use to declare it to the whole world.

Things to expire	Deadline	How will you declare it?

Intelligence v/s Wisdom

There are two important elements in this process of self-expiration — Intelligence and Wisdom. Intelligence is when you have an ***understanding*** of a particular concept; for instance you know how to sell; whereas wisdom is when you have ***implemented*** that knowledge in your life and have gained mastery over that subject, i.e. you've mastered the art of selling. Intelligence is all about knowing, whereas wisdom is about doing what you know, over and over again, experimenting with it, innovating, renovating, and continuously repeating it till such time that you gain mastery over it and are able to guarantee results in that arena.

Don't people know that they should get up early in the morning, go for a walk, exercise for some time, read a book to upgrade their knowledge, grow their business year-on-year, not procrastinate, and so on. But does everyone do that?

Don't consider yourself any less intelligent if you are something like this. As I've said earlier, the question is not about intelligence, but of wisdom. Everybody has the same amount of intelligence, but few are able to take the lead in the journey of life while the rest keep wondering why 'they' and why not 'we'? The answer to this is very simple — those who surge ahead operate from their wisdom while the others are still playing at the level of intelligence.

Intelligence and Wisdom — these two words bring to my mind two very well known names in the world of Indian cricket — Sachin Tendulkar who is the darling batsman of India and Vinod Kambli who could have given Sachin some serious competition, but faded after a guest appearance in the world of cricket. Both entered the game at the same time, with the same passion and zest. Kambli had a lot more talent and flair, compared to Tendulkar. But he ended up being the 'intelligent' man whereas Sachin took the lead with his 'wisdom' and has been thriving for the last 24 years. That is wisdom! And it only comes to people who think beyond their intelligence.

Life's tragedy is that we get old too soon and wise too late.
~ Benjamin Franklin.

Don't let this tragedy happen to you. To think beyond intelligence and become wise, it is imperative that you practise the virtue of continuously expiring your current self, as wisdom can only be gathered when you keep rising to the next level.

Wisdom Manufacturing Process

Having said that 'Life Maximization' can only happen if you operate from the level of wisdom, the next question is how can wisdom be attained? Well, first and foremost we all need to understand that wisdom is not an external element that can be attained, it is an intrinsic component that needs to be manufactured from within yourself and this process is known as the Wisdom Manufacturing Process.

The Wisdom Manufacturing Process has four steps :

1. Data
2. Information
3. Knowledge
4. Wisdom

Step 1 — Data

Data is what we acquire from books, audios, videos, friends, training programmes, etc. About 95% of this data is forgotten within 24 hours and the next 5% is gone in a week. When you read a book on sales or leadership, or listen to an audiobook, you acquire some data. If this data is not converted into information, it is lost forever.

Cosmetic changes certainly take place when you read a book and most people feel overwhelmed, excited and exhilarated, but that is where their story with the book ends. Life Maximizers, on the other hand, don't stop at Step 1! They take it to the next level and that is information.

Step 2 — Information

The next step in the Wisdom Manufacturing Process is to convert data into information. This art is practised differently by each person. Someone may record whatever he/she has understood from a training process. Another Life Maximizer may repeat the entire process a hundred times to strengthen his/her understanding of it. Your preferred method of conversion could be entirely different.

My mechanism in the last 29 years has been applying my understanding and intellect to the data gathered and then writing over a 100 pages about each book that I read, audio or video that I go through or training programme that I attend, thus putting it in black and white for future reference. As you acquire more and more data and convert it into information, you expire your current self and rise to the next level. Therefore, the decision to expire your current self and renew it begins here.

Step 3 — Knowledge

After converting data into information, you need to persistently put this information into practice and once this is done regularly, it becomes your knowledge. Knowledge is the stage of implementation. When you practise what you have decided, you will fail miserably since your old self keeps fighting the new self while attempting to do something different.

You fail, fail, fail, fail, and fail continuously, but you still persist. You go back to your information to see where are you failing and how can you correct yourself. After correcting yourself several times, gradually the frequency of the failure starts reducing (as depicted in the diagram above) and you finally touch success for the first time. This is where you rise one step ahead of knowledge and enter the last stage of this process.

Step 4 — Wisdom

After increasing your efforts, you may finally succeed in doing the new action correctly, but then the cycle of failure may start again. However, when failure turns into repeated success, the size of the success starts becoming larger and more prominent and it is here that knowledge finally turns into wisdom.

At this stage you know what exactly needs to be done; what characteristics are required to win a difficult situation; how to treat someone who is a celebrated liar and transform him/her into a truthful person; and so on. This is where you have manufactured wisdom within yourself in all these areas.

Wisdom when manufactured stays forever and a person who gains wisdom on a particular subject becomes the king of that subject.

I remember when I first attended a programme by Don Beverage, I wrote down everything that the world-renowned Life Coach had said throughout the day, elaborating the precise notes that I had made, thus converting my data into information. Not only did I jot down what I had understood, but I also wrote what I learnt from his words and the benefits I could derive from it. While I was converting this data into information, I gave myself the commandment that I would implement everything I have learnt today, chapter-by-chapter in my life, and charted an action plan to achieve this target. I also purchased the manuscript and with my notes I imbibed every learning into my most unconscious psyche. With great pride and thrill I can tell you that till today, 20 years later, I practise every word written in that book.

In the 1990s, I attended a programme called 'LIFE — Living in Freedom and Enquiry' and a seven-day sequel called 'The Existential Laboratory' conducted by Swami Sukhabodhananda in a residential camp surrounded by greenery. We stayed in tents and didn't have electricity at night. I went against the rules of the workshop that strictly prohibited any participant from staying awake beyond a certain time in the evening, and I covered myself with a bedsheet and for hours I wrote down my key takeaways from the day-long course, thus converting the data that I acquired into information. And today those learnings have become my deep-rooted wisdom!

I jotted down my thoughts when I attended the MILT Leadership Course and the MILT Sales Course by Aporesh Acharya, Dianetics by Helmut Flasch, and other such programmes. The audiobook on goal setting by Zig Ziglar which I heard in 1985, various books by Tom Hopkins, Brian Tracy, Zig Ziglar, Dan Sullivan that I have read over the years and the audios and videos of Joel Barker that I have been an ardent follower of, are all present in my study in the form of heaps and heaps of pages I wrote about each one of them. Today they are all part of my wisdom!

In the table given below, write down four key learnings that you have gained from the above concept, the actions you will take to permanently imbibe it in your life along with the deadlines and the help you will require.

No.	Learnings	Actions you will take to imbibe this in your life	Whose help will you require	Deadline
1				
2				
3				
4				

The best way to learn is to teach. Speak about this concept to every human being you meet over the next one week and see if you can introduce this term 'Declare your expiry date' in your vocabulary.

One needs to manufacture wisdom in all aspects of life, i.e. sales, leadership, marketing, branding, team building, people management, punctuality, behaviour, personality, the way you dress, walk, talk, etc. and all areas of your personal and professional interest. When you operate from your wisdom, you will be able to expire your current self and keep renewing it from time-to-time, thus rising to the next level.

In order to maximize life for a lifetime, you need to give this order, this instruction, this directive, this mandate, this law of God, this commandment everyday, every hour, every minute of your life —

Declare your expiry date!

COMMANDMENT

2

Be a possibility thinker

Possibility is what you don't know.

Be a possibility thinker, not a positive thinker!

- → Possibility is the unknown.
- → It is beyond imagination, intention, and comprehension.
- → It is beyond the immediate, beyond your present thoughts, words, and deeds.
- → Possibility is what does not currently exist in any form — thought or idea.
- → It is the creation of a whole new world. A world of possibilities.
- → It is the belief to do what you've never done before; create what never existed before.
- → *Possibility is pure; it is God; it is what will surprise the world and leave it awestruck.*

You may be a positive thinker, but positive thinking stops when circumstances and conditions around you start changing. Life can never be maximized by positive thinkers because they become negative when things go wrong, situations get out of control and the world leaves you mid-way to fend for yourself, to solve things on your own.

To be a Life Maximizer, you need to be a Possibility Thinker!

Have you ever attempted something that seemed beyond imagination? For example, growing your business by 500% in one year, cutting down your weight by 20 kg in one month, shifting your well established business from one city to the other overnight and while doing so, did you have to face ridicule and mockery? If not, then you haven't explored the impossible yet.

Thomas Edison failed over 10,000 times while attempting to make an electric bulb, but he never gave up; Narayan Murthy failed innumerable times while attempting to build Infosys; Ray Kroc faced rejection from over 300 investors for his idea of McDonalds; Kishore Biyani faced opposition from his own family while revolutionizing the retail industry through Big Bazaar; Walt Disney was mocked by the world when he unveiled his idea of Disneyland, but not one of them ever gave up. They persisted and persisted till they converted their dreams into realities. They were all Possibility Thinkers.

So what is it that distinguishes Possibility Thinkers from ordinary mortals? The sole discriminator is that Possibility Thinkers operate from the theory of no constraints — constraints of time, money, resources, etc. do not exist for them and they find alternate ways of doing things, irrespective of any worldly, or unworldly limitations.

One may not have the best facilities, resources, money, and time to deliver the required outcome. And in such a situation declaring that something cannot be done is the easiest thing to do; an act of utter common sense that does not require any thinking at all. But still delivering the required outcome despite all these restrictions requires not just thinking or positive thinking, but possibility thinking and this is what makes a person a possibility thinker.

For example, you may be asked to organise a party/event within a certain budget, within 24 hours, with no aid or assistance. Or, you may be given a target of manufacturing 1000 units a day from a facility that until then produced only 350 units. An ordinary person would instantly say 'This is impossible to do, I cannot do it'. But a Possibility Thinker will explore how it can be done rather than debating whether it can be done or not.

Yet, our middle-route guys between the impossibility and the possibility thinkers — the 'Positive Thinkers' when faced with the pressure of 1000 units, with the fear of not letting down the people assigning this task, will agree to do the impossible by declaring one or all of the following strong statements:

1. Let's be realistic.
2. Let's be practical.
3. I will try my best.

He may start by saying, 'This is not realistic, this is not practical, but even so, if you insist I will try my level best to do it'. In the dialogue itself, he has made a provision to fail and the irony is that this failure also gives him the satisfaction and the courage to stand with his head held high — after all, he *tried!*

But Possibility Thinkers don't make such statements. They just get on with the task and do it, evoking their deepest capabilities and abilities and the abilities of their ecosystem. As it is said, the true character and calibre of a person emerges only when he/she is pushed to the limits, the theory of no constraints ensures that when people are pushed beyond their limit, their true worth is tested and Life Maximizers are created out of ordinary mortals. Either you will emerge, or you will renounce. There is no third way out.

If you get everything on a platter, the need to work under the theory of no constraints never occurs. I consider myself extremely lucky for not having all the wealth and the riches of the world on my side as this forced me to work within constraints through the last 29 years, thus making me a Possibility Thinker.

I remember 12 years ago, in 2000, when I set out to start my own training company, I didn't even have a place to set up my office. I started off **smm**art from the garden of my father's one-room kitchen home along with a colleague and from there built it to what it is today. Had I been too overwhelmed with the constraints of money and resources that life posed at me back then, **smm**art would have never happened and I would still be working for another company.

And who says that there are no constraints today? Well, of course there are constraints. There are constraints of time, body, resources, money, and there always will be. Though I have fairly reasonable riches in my life today, I have trained my mind, body, heart, and soul to operate like a Possibility Thinker till my last breath, thus I will be in a position to take on higher challenges in life, unlike my other friends and colleagues who at this age and stature in life, despite all the riches, facilities, and resources around them, start to decelerate, dissipate, disintegrate, and stop moving forward. They get into a safety zone and life maximization stops for them, right then and there.

Possibility thinking has no connection with age, health, and wealth of an individual. It is a game of the mind, for the mind, in the mind; a permanent phenomenon which only ends with life.

In my life as a trainer, I have come across a lot of people who feel very strongly about working out, focusing on their health, reading and upgrading themselves, undergoing a training programme etc. but get bogged down by the paucity of time and give up. For an ordinary man, coming home at 7 pm, watching two hours of television, having dinner with the family and retiring to bed by 10.30 is the norm.

But in case of Possibility Thinkers, the idea that you have to go home in the evening, eat on time, watch television, sleep at night, rest, etc. does not even occur. They very deliberately decide that these are things meant for ordinary mortals and if they have to be different from the world and maximize life, this pattern needs to be redesigned. And so, they never face paucity of time if they want to work out, read a book, or attend a training programme. They can get up at three in the morning and practise yoga, go for a walk, organise a day-and-night training programme. Morning or evening, early or late, day or night does not matter to them until they have achieved what they have set out for.

In our mythologies and legends and even in today's newspapers, we've heard of Possibility Thinkers. Take for instance, Eklavya in *Mahabharata*, A.P.J. Abdul Kalam, Dadasaheb Phalke and Mother Teresa.

For Eklavya, it was learning the art of archery that Dronacharya was not ready to teach him. But the Possibility Thinker within Eklavya did not allow him to give up, despite not having a tutor. Instead, he worked out alternate ways of learning the art and became a better archer than the tutored Arjun.

A.P.J. Abdul Kalam did not permit poverty to subdue his ambitions, he studied under streetlights and purely due to his achievements and knowledge was appointed the President of India.

Dadasaheb Phalke is considered to be the greatest contributor to Indian cinema. Hailing from an ordinary family, living an ordinary life amidst ordinary situations and circumstances, running his own printing press, the only thing extraordinary about this legendary man was his dream of making the first Indian film and setting the stage for the entire film industry in India. With poverty on one side and absolute lack of knowledge about film-making on the other, the possibility thinker in Dadasaheb Phalke defied all laws and conditions to chase his dream.

From closing down his printing press to withstanding extreme financial ruin and pledging his wife's jewellery, he went to England and studied film technology, bought the necessary equipment and started his virtual factory here, in India. When no woman was ready to face the camera and the consequent social stigma, he cast a cook's feminine-looking male assistant as his heroine, but did not give up in the absence of a lead actor. In this period, he almost lost his eyesight due to the excessive strain caused by film viewing, underwent severe physical, mental, financial and emotional ordeals, came on the streets, sold everything that he had including cutlery, did everything except for one thing — give up!

He was obsessed with his belief in making the first motion picture in India and there was nobody between him and God. His belief, passion, and purpose gave us the gift of the 'Indian Film Industry'. He did not succumb to the constraints surrounding him, but persisted till he achieved his dream and left a permanent mark on the Indian film fraternity and will be remembered for as long as life exists on earth.

Far away from this iconic film maker, in another century, in another part of the world, were two young boys with the same zest, zeal, and passion to create something that never existed. In 1998, 25-year-olds Sergey Brin and Larry Page suspended their Ph. D. studies at Stanford University to create an online search engine called 'Google'. They reformed the internet by innovating something called 'Search Engine Optimization' — a concept that was unheard of, unseen, non-existent and from there made Google a household name in less than a decade. No rules/regulations/norms or even case study existed to guide these two young brains. They created their own patterns, directed themselves and have created a mammoth organisation that continues to influence modern technology.

Whether it was Neeraj Gupta who transformed the conventional black-and-yellow taxis into sophisticated air-conditioned radio cabs called Meru now available across many cities in India, and even more importantly transformed the rogue, brash, manipulative, uncivilised and unionised local taxi drivers into well-mannered, refined and cultured chauffeurs; or Mark Zuckerberg who took the internet by storm by creating a powerful social networking website called Facebook; whether it was the idea of Starbucks Coffee of creating a third home for the youth or the recent Tutor Vista, a Bengaluru-based coaching academy run by husband-wife Suresh and Mina Krishnan, teaching students in the US, UK and abroad their school curriculum through the internet — all of these are innovative creations in their own right.

Neither of them had any antecedent to refer to, patterns to follow, models to observe, example to learn from, or any guide to point towards the right path. They guided themselves, directed their own actions, carved their own paths, created possibility from impossibilities, and maximized life for themselves and millions around. They were guided by only one aim — create something that never existed before!

'It's kind of fun to do the impossible.'
~ Walt Disney

Moving from impossibility to possibility thinking

To be a Possibility Thinker, the fundamental question you need to ask yourself is something I learnt from Joel Barker, the great guru of change, many years ago:

If there is something that is impossible to do in my business today, and it could be done, would it fundamentally change what I do?

Though this question talks about the impossible that you achieve in your business, you can apply this question to your life as well by framing it as expressed here:

If there is something that is impossible to do in my life today, and it could be done, would it fundamentally change what I do?

Ask this question innumerable times, tweak it, twist it, play with it and create multiple variants of it:

If there is something that is impossible to do with my husband/wife/kids/parents, relationships, and it could be done, would it fundamentally change what I do?

If there is something that is impossible to do in my business/market/territory, and it could be done, would it fundamentally change what I do?

If there is something that is impossible to do with my time, and it could be done, would it fundamentally change what I do?

If there is something that is impossible to do with my money, and it could be done, would it fundamentally change what I do?

If there is something that is impossible to do with my body, and it could be done, would it fundamentally change what I do?

When you ask yourself the 'Possibility Thinker Question' and then actually do the impossible, the world around you starts taking notice of you and Life Maximization begins. When you do a series of impossible things, the world starts observing you, following you, idealizing you and Life Maximization regularises within you; the process of Life Maximization institutionalizes within you.

From an ordinary human being, you now start becoming a public figure, the pressure starts mounting on you — remember the public pressure we mentioned in Chapter 1 — and you start seeing the world from an altogether different perspective — one that you never knew existed within you. Everything that you now think, communicate, and do will change the world for the better and your existence on this planet suddenly becomes meaningful. The world starts looking at you for direction, guidance, and motivation. You say goodbye to the Wandering Generality that you were, and enter the zone of the Meaningful Specific. You now become a Life Maximizer!

I joined Eureka Forbes on 4 October, 1985 as a door-to-door salesman selling vacuum cleaners. In those days, the national sales average of Eureka Forbes for a month was four vacuum cleaners and there were people who did a maximum of 8, 12, or 14. There were rare cases of 20 in a month also, but this was not sustained.

On 11 October 1985, with just 20 days left for the closing of the month, I sold 26 vacuum cleaners and marked the spectacular start of my journey as a salesman. Next month I sold 32 vacuum cleaners, 33 sales in the following month, then 34, 36, 39, 41, 43. The numbers went on increasing month-on-month.

Our then All India Sales Head, Mr. Anil Ambo who was my boss's superior would always say that a successful salesman should sell at least one more than the previous month. I took this very seriously and never sold less than my previous month ever, throughout my sales career. Impossible to do, but I did it. I was a Possibility Thinker!

For the first time in the history of Eureka Forbes, a branch posted 300 sales, this was my branch; I was the first Branch Manager to complete 400 sales in a month and then 500 sales in a month; an enormously tall order — nobody dared to undertake it;

nobody even dared to think about it. Impossible to do, but I did it. I was a Possibility Thinker!

Throughout my eight glorious years at Eureka Forbes, I did what no other salesman, Group Leader, Sales Supervisor, Branch Manager, Divisional Sales Manager, ever did. There has never been a salesman, sales manager, or a sales leader like me that the company has ever had till date. The records I made still stand uncontested and are aspirational for all new entrants at Eureka. When I left Eureka Forbes, I was the youngest, fastest growing, richest employee in the history of the organisation. Impossible to leave such a lasting mark, but I did it. I was a Possibility Thinker!

In Real Value, the second company that I worked for after bidding goodbye to Eureka Forbes, I was doing very well as a Deputy General Manager, breaking all past and present records month after month till the other division of our company called the Vacuumizer Division collapsed taking the company to the stage of BIFR (Board of Industrial & Financial Restructuring). The company was unable to pay salaries on time; payments to vendors and suppliers were deferred and we had to ask people to leave while some left on their own. It was a difficult situation.

Amidst this deterioration, Pradeep Patil, my colleague and Branch Manager and I decided to recruit a group of rejected candidates and built a team to start afresh. This was not normal. We had never done this before. We didn't like doing it. But we didn't want to give up; we wanted to win. So we built a team of 20 rejected candidates that neither of us would have hired during normal times and transformed them into performers. We did not blame the situation, circumstance, or constraints of money and resources. Impossible to do, but we did it. We were Possibility Thinkers!

And this stint of transforming rejected candidates into performers went on to become one of the most fulfilling experiences of my life, for it instilled in me an enduring belief that any kind of person can be turned around, irrespective of his degrees and accolades. So when you walk into any of our **smm**art offices you will never see anyone — from our office assistants to the receptionist, drivers, front line sales executives or senior level manager — doing the same job the next time you walk in. Impossible to do, but I did it and continue doing it. I am a Possibility Thinker!

I started my journey in the field of training and consultancy in 1996 and I would keep asking myself the 'Possibility Thinker Question' quite often, back then, *If there is something that is impossible to do as a trainer, and it could be done, would it fundamentally change what I do?*

And I once said to myself, it is impossible to do 10 days of training, 10 days of business development and 10 days of planning, preparation, and self-upgradation in a single month. I set that as my target and did it. Then, I increased it to 15 days of training, 20 days of training and where all my trainer friends dreaded over 8-10 days of travel, I remember a month where I was in a position to comfortably execute over 24 days of continuous training programmes, travelling through the nights and preparing while travelling, without feeling the pinch of any physical, mental or psychological exertion on my mind or body. Impossible to do, but I did it. I was a Possibility Thinker!

As a salesman I had pledged to myself that I would never go home until I had sold at least one vacuum cleaner a day. One day, in 1986, I had knocked hundreds of doors and given my sales presentation to many people, but it was 11.45 pm and I had not yet sold a single vacuum cleaner. I had promised myself I would not go home without a sale. This was my policy/punishment in life and I wanted to stick to it. At about a few minutes to midnight, I saw a light on the second floor of a building. I went to that house and knocked on the door without even thinking for a moment.

The man who opened the door looked shocked and surprised to see a salesman at that hour. Without allowing that shock to register, I started my sales pitch, 'Sir, I am from Eureka Forbes and I have a small machine with me which can clean everything in your house from top to bottom. I'd like to give you a no-obligation, free demonstration. Can I come in Sir?' The man interrupted me and said, 'Gentleman, it is midnight.' And I said, 'Yes Sir, it is midnight. Can I come in?'

I knew what that man meant to say. But I refused to be constrained by his thoughts of time and so I continued my pitch. He then asked me why was I working so hard and I told him there are two reasons for this:

1. I wanted to become a Big Man

2. I had promised myself not to go home until I sold at least one vacuum cleaner every day.

He allowed me in and I gave him a stunning presentation. He was impressed and said that he would buy four pieces. I was surprised and excited at the same time; here I was struggling to sell one and this man said he wanted to buy four. I asked him why four and he told me, 'I run luxury busses between Mumbai and Mahabaleshwar (a hill station in Maharashtra) and have four buses in my fleet. When people travel, they drop wafers, peanuts etc. in the bus. Can this vacuum cleaner suck that in and clean the bus?' I said yes, it would and he said, in that case he would like to buy four machines.

His buses generally returned to Mumbai by 10-11pm; but on that particular day one of the buses had broken down and they were delayed by a few hours. He was awake at midnight because his vehicles were expected to reach the designated stop by 1.30 am and he was just getting ready to go there. I went along with him to Marine Drive where they were to arrive and waited there till about 3.30 am when the bus finally came.

I jumped in and started the demonstration and to my surprise and horror, the machine just didn't start because of some battery problem in the bus. The demo failed and the man refused to buy the machines. I understood that my test was still unfinished.

He asked me if he could drop me somewhere, and I said Mahalaxmi Station. We got there at about 4 am. The first train would arrive at 4.30 am and take me either to South Mumbai where my sales territory was (Grant Road) or to North Mumbai where I resided (Andheri). It did not even occur to me to board the train that would go home and I took the train that would take me to my sales territory. I bought a toothbrush and toothpaste, freshened up at a hotel, which opened early in the morning to cater to the mill workers in the area and even before the influx of the mill workers, I opened my account at both these places that day and here I was, ready for my field work as usual.

I reached my territory at 6.45 am (the time I generally started my day knocking on doors, making cold calls, fixing appointments for the same day, next day, or next-to-next day). I sold three vacuum cleaners by 12 pm, as vengeance for the previous night, I deposited the payments in the office and went home. I had promised myself that I wouldn't go home unless I sold one vacuum cleaner per day and I kept my promise. Impossible to do, but I did it. I was a Possibility Thinker!

Salespersons generally start their day at 9.30-10 am and would start fieldwork only by 11 am. I reached my territory everyday by 6.45 am and finished 25-30% of my work by 9 am where the rest of world was just preparing to start. I was ahead of the world by 25-

30% and I realised that if you make it a habit to be ahead of others by 25-30%, then over 8-10 years, your life starts maximizing. I did not know it then, but I know it now.

List the 12 things that are impossible to do in your business, (or life, relationship, field, discipline, market, department, technology, product, etc… just pick one), but if it could be done in the next one year, would it fundamentally change what you do?

____

____

____

____

____

____

____

____

____

____

____

____

____

____

As I said at the beginning of this chapter, possibility is what you don't know, what is beyond your imagination, intention, and comprehension; beyond current thoughts, words and deeds. It is 'meaningless' when you are doing it but 'meaningful' after you have done it. So if you believe something is impossible, don't hesitate, just do it. Over a period of time, this possibility will become your second nature and nature endures; nature thrives in difficulties; nature never gives up!

You become god-like when you do the impossible. You become a Possibility Thinker!

In order to maximize life for a lifetime, you need to give this order, this instruction, this directive, this mandate, this law of God, this commandment every day, every hour, every minute of your life:

Be a possibility thinker.

3

Rock the boat in the middle of the sea

The life of a non-life maximizer is solidly comfortable.
And comfort kills Life Maximization.

We live in discontinuous and uncertain times. On a daily, hourly basis, new ideas, products and services are launched. If you don't launch it someone else will; if you don't bring in new ideas, someone else will; if you don't introduce new products and services, the credit will go to another; if you don't take up challenges, they will be taken up by others; if you don't go to Mount Everest to conquer it, it will be conquered by another... whoever goes first would have maximized life!

Each time someone else moves forward and conquers the world, you can only express regret, be upset, feel miserable, and small. You can then be a follower and survive. However, if you want be a leader and thrive, not survive, you have to rock the boat in the middle of the sea.

This means challenging the status quo, doing things differently, questioning the present, disrupting the apple cart, changing the wheels of your car while you are driving it! It means doing things when everything is fine; experimenting when there is no obvious need to do so; doing something to test the next possibility. It means permanently staying ahead and not allowing others to catch up with you.

Rock the boat when you are in the middle of the sea, not at the shore!

When you rock the boat on or near the shore, it may shake a little but then quickly stabilise before you begin your journey. But when you rock the boat in the middle of the sea, it can lead to grave consequences — the boat may turn around, the water may start seeping in, the passengers could drown, and life and resources could be destroyed.

Connect this analogy to the boat of life. Having reached the peak of your business/career, when everything is going well, life is steady, revenues are flowing in, productivity is at its best, people may not want to shake things, experiment, innovate, switch a job, shift the industry, change the line of business, products, model of operation etc. and disrupt the status quo because they are scared of the consequences. They are content with their current success, stature, name, fame and wealth and do not want to lose what is already there to pursue bigger dreams. Some fear rocking the boat because of their age, some because of the risk it involves and some due to the hardships they have already suffered in life to get to wherever they are today.

But very few people know that the only thing that will take them to the next step on the ladder of fame, success and wealth is rocking the boat of life in the middle of the sea. Those who know this, maximize life!

Why is this essential? When you are successful, a certain arrogant attitude sets in. You start believing the future is merely an extension of the past, that the ideas that have pulled you this far are the same ideas that will take you to your future. You feel what you are thinking, doing and acting is the only way of achieving your goals and a paradigm is formed.

Your national pastime now is to convince the whole world that what you are doing is right and you become blind to the possibilities of life. You become old, get into a state of captivity, a state of mind where you eternally wait for things to happen. You become physically and mentally tired, lose your beauty, radiance, fire and zest for life. Your ability to hunt goes astray and you get entrenched in your daily routines. You lose your understanding of the importance of stealth and ambush, toughness, you let go of your edge over life and the ability to exploit your full potential and the full potential of your ecosystem. Your sense of timing and territory is lost and you become dependent and inward looking. Your ability to guard yourself goes for a toss and you get caged in your beliefs.

You enter into a state of inertia, a state of drunken bliss and this is an indicator of failure!

One of the commandments that I gave myself to disassociate from such a state of mind was:

Rock the boat of life in the middle of the sea!

When you set out to rock the boat, you must keep in mind four ground rules, either or all of which will lead you to maximization:

1. Believe in the philosophy of discontinuity
2. Do not ask for a guarantee
3. Do not look for endorsements from others
4. Rock the boat when you are at the peak of success

Believe in the Philosophy of Discontinuity

Nothing in life is permanent. The people around you — their commitment, support, dedication; your relationships and their longevity; the nature of your present job/business, income, circumstances, standard of living, wealth, comfort, struggle; and life itself. Nothing is eternal/continuous. It has to come to an end someday, it has to discontinue.

Many people are paralysed by their current state of affairs and feel it will be consistent through their life. They fear disrupting the status quo. But as it is rightly said, unless you leave the familiar behind, you will never be able to reach newer heights and to do this, one needs to embrace the philosophy of discontinuity. In organisations, this philosophy of discontinuity must be institutionalized at all levels. Every person, relationship, product, process, system, model, methodology and perhaps the entire business may need to be discontinued from time-to-time and something new needs to be infused. When you discontinue the current practices and move into a new industry, you may fail miserably, but you have to be prepared for this failure, face it, fight it, and emerge victorious.

Bajaj Auto of the Bajaj Group, the house that produces motorcycles like Pulsar, Discover, etc. was once recognised as a scooter manufacturer. It took an entire decade for Bajaj Auto to convey its transformation into a two-wheeler manufacturer, with a great line of motorcycles and bikes. The only thought guiding them was the Philosophy of Discontinuity.

Back then, their flagship product was Bajaj Chetak, the household name for a two-wheeler scooter. A maverick called Rajeev Bajaj decided to change this identity. When the world's largest motorcycle manufacturers, the likes of Hero Motocorp, Yamaha etc., were venturing into scooters, he decided to retract from the scooter business and become a 100% motorcycle manufacturing brand.

His father, Rahul Bajaj, was his foremost critic and eternal opponent, but Rajeev held fort for he knew that unless he discontinued his existent product, he would never be able to create his niche. Thus, with discontinuity as his guiding light, he rocked the boat and with its wide range of bikes today, Bajaj Auto is a renowned motorcycle player, with operations in over 50 countries all over the world.

Similarly, Nokia, a leading brand in the telecommunication sector was originally a manufacturer of pulp and paper. It was founded as Nokia Company in 1865 in a small town of the same name in central Finland. As technology advanced and forest activities reduced, Nokia realised that if it continued in the same industry it would be wiped off in no time. So, from a forest management company, it reinvented itself as a telecommunication giant. If Nokia has to still surge ahead and rule the world as a business house, it will have to go back to the philosophy of discontinuity once again. This could be discontinuity of a certain thought process within the telecommunication industry or discontinuing from the telecommunication industry itself to venture into something new, different, and better that will take it to its next level.

ITC is another great example. As the name suggests, Indian Tobacco Company (formerly known as the Imperial Tobacco Company of India) was a leading producer of cigarettes way back in the early 1970s. With rising awareness about the negative effects of tobacco and cigarette consumption, the then chief Ajit Haskar knew that if ITC stayed solely in the tobacco business, it would soon hit the wall. In 1975 itself, ITC spread its wings and went on a diversification spree, marking its presence in hotels, paperboards and specialty papers, packaging, agri-business, packaged foods and confectionery, information technology, branded apparel, personal care, stationery, safety matches, and other FMCG products. With an annual turnover of over $7 billion and 26,000 employees spread over 60 locations, today, ITC Ltd. has earned its reputation as a diversified business house.

Formed in 1955, ICICI Bank was then known as the Industrial Credit and Investment Corporation of India — a joint venture between the World Bank, India's public sector banks and public sector insurance companies to provide project financing to the Indian industry. It ran as a conservative unit till the 1990s, which is when K.V. Kamath took over as the MD and CEO after an eight-year tenure in Asian Development Bank, Manila. Kamath knew that the Indian banking sector was quickly evolving and if they continued in the sphere of project financing, they would become a lost name. He therefore transformed the entity from a development financial institution offering only project finance to a diversified financial services group, offering a wide variety of products and services and opened its doors to retail customers.

He initiated a series of acquisitions of non-banking finance companies in 1996-98 and led the way to the formation of ICICI Bank. ICICI Bank launched internet banking operations in 1998 and by then had completely rebranded itself as a one-stop financial services provider. In 1999, they become the first Indian company and the first bank or financial institution from non-Japan Asia to be listed on the NYSE and in 2000, it became the first Indian bank to be listed on the New York Stock Exchange with its five million American depository shares issue generating a demand book 13 times the offer size.

Discontinuity is necessary!

Do not ask for a guarantee

Guarantee, assurance, safety, security, are all words meant for ordinary mortals. Life Maximizers do not ask for a guarantee before taking on new initiatives.

They don't need to be sure that the risk they are taking will work for them and not take them down the drain; that a new job will bring growth; a new book will be accepted; a new design will be approved; a new tune will become popular; a new place will bring fortune; a new product will sell; a new employee will perform; a new process will improve productivity; a new market will increase the business; a new model will enhance profitability, and so on.

They believe in doing things. They take risks; they take risky decisions and then make them happen for each of these risks are well thought of, calculated risks. And this is not merely because they are optimistic about the future, but because they know that even if they fail, they have the courage and the capacity to steer away from these debacles; for what drives them is their passion.

Life Maximizers are passionate about what they do.

Passion is when you are committed to something with no guarantee of any return.

~ Dan Sullivan

Steve Jobs was committed to the cause of innovation without being bothered about the name, fame, and prosperity the products would fetch him and kept introducing the most unbelievable technology ever. A. R. Rahman is committed to the world of music without any expectations from the audience and so comes a *Jai Ho* or *Sadda Haq* (two of the most popular and top ranking Hindi songs he has created). There is always a chance that *Sadda Haq* may fall on its face or an iPhone 4 may collapse, but then what drives these men is the passion for excellence and not the need for success.

When an INR 2500 crore company called iGATE bought a INR 5000 crore conglomerate called Patni — double the size of its buyer — Phaneesh Murthy rocked the boat in the middle of the sea. He had no guarantee that this union would work; that he would be able to integrate the two companies; that the veterans at Patni would stay put; that the stock market would be by their side; that iGATE will be able to sustain this purchase; that they will not go bankrupt; that they will succeed….

He was just passionate about his business and that passion forced him to pursue this tie-up. Phaneesh Murthy maximized life — for himself, iGATE, and Patni Computers.

No Endorsements

Life Maximizers are loners in their journey. They are self-contained, self-sufficient, independent individuals who are confident of their actions and work with their solitary thought process, independent of support, backing, or approval of the world in doing what they feel is right. They have a mind of their own — an intuition, a gut feeling, a well thought, well researched judgment which directs them towards their future and they do not need the endorsement of the external world to take on newer initiatives. Not seeking endorsements is not an act of arrogance, but Life Maximizers know that their ideas will be shot down by the world and they will be asked to toe the line with the philosophies that the world believes in. Their wisdom tells them that the people around them will not even be able to comprehend their idea, let alone believe in them or support them and yet these are ideas that can change the world and hence, they do not rely on public approval to make their move.

They are rebels, rebels with a cause — the cause can be innovation; it can be freedom; it can be the cause for a nation, a community, a company; and the cause is so strong and powerful that they can take it and run with it without seeking endorsement from anyone else. They break the rules and norms of the world, believe in taking chances, do what they feel is right in pursuit of exploring what life has in store for them and do not get bogged down by their loneliness, isolation, and lack of patronage.

They are leaders and they know that they will always be alone while rocking the boat and the world will only come along once the boat is steady and is ready to lead them to the new path of Life Maximization. And though they will cross this path together, Life Maximizers will always be looked upon as 'pioneers' and the ordinary mortals as 'their followers.'

Azim Premji, the Chairman of Wipro, one of India's largest IT companies — fired two of his CEOs recently on grounds of slowing down growth. This could have led to multiple other resignations within the company, the stock prices could have gone for a toss, it could have triggered gossip and rumours in the market and led to bad-mouthing and disgrace in the industry. But Azim Premji knew what he was doing and he was prepared for all these consequences for he knew that these things were bound to happen. He was rocking the boat in the middle of the sea and was not seeking the approval of the world and hence recorded a profit of INR 1456.40 crore — an 11.95% increase in the last quarter of the financial year 2011-12 (during which he played this gigantic move). He is a Life Maximizer!

Write down five decisions that you will take in your personal and professional life over the next one year, based on your gut feeling, courage, and intuition, without seeking the support or endorsement of others and construct an action plan with deadlines:

No.	Decisions	Deadline	Action plan
1			
2			
3			
4			
5			

Do it at the peak of success

If one has to rock the boat, it needs to be done at the peak of success!

Hundreds and thousands of businesses dwindle because they are overwhelmed with their market leadership, they are unable to anticipate that the rest of the world will dethrone them if they do not change now.

India's first ever successful car — the Ambassador (manufactured by Hindustan Motors) ruled the Indian automobile industry for a very long period, but could not sustain its position when Maruti and the other players came up with lighter, more fashionable, smaller and sleeker cars and Ambassador became history.

Doordarshan — the first ever Indian TV channel that enjoyed supreme monopoly suddenly collapsed when Star TV and other satellite channels came into being.

In the 1960s, and even before that, Switzerland was regarded as the world's largest watch manufacturing country. Their technology was automatic watches — something that they had mastered over many years and had paid back more than substantial returns. Their market share was more than 65% and they were considered as the uncontested leaders in the watchmaking arena. 'Made in Switzerland' meant rich, classy, and adhering to extremely high standards. Life was beautiful; the Swiss were rising; they were at the peak of success. In 1968, a group of watch researchers approached the topmost Swiss watch manufacturers and presented a new technology for manufacturing watches — the Quartz technology. It had lesser components and was a thousand times more accurate than the automatic watches. According to watch researchers, this would be the future of the watch industry!

The idea was instantly rejected as the Swiss believed that it could not add any value to the watch industry. They believed that the future would be an extension of the past and were blind to the idea of electronic watches. So confident were they about their belief that they did not even protect the idea by patenting it under their name and allowed the researchers to go unacknowledged.

Rejected by the Swiss watchmakers, the researchers did not give up hope. They believed in their idea; they were rebels with a cause; they wanted to give something that was technologically more advanced and worthwhile to their industry. They were on the lookout for someone who would accept their idea and that same year went to the Annual Watch Congress and to exhibit their technology. Two companies — Seiko in Japan and Texas Instruments in USA, were interested in taking it forward and the rest is history.

Exactly ten years later, in 1978, the Swiss lost their position as market leader to the Japanese and came down from 65% market share to merely 10% market share worldwide. And so dramatic was the impact of this descent that they had to let go of 50,000 of their 65,000 watch workers. A nation at the peak of success could have continued higher by rocking the boat in the middle of the sea and accepting, appreciating, and adopting a new technology, but it fell prey to pride and the inability to recognise a new idea and dwindled so quickly that it could never rise up again. If you don't change direction when at the peak, it won't be long before you are thrown down to the ground.

If only Ambassador, Doordarshan, and Swiss watch companies had anticipated this revolution and changed before time!

Change before you have to

Any change brings with it a lot of fear, insecurities, difficulties, pain, sacrifice, and risk. When you are at the crest of success and decide to change, you don't feel the difficulty or the pain because the change that you are initiating is largely self-driven and self-initiated. It is not driven by the market. It is not forced upon you. If a change is forced, half your energy and passion is lost in resisting the change; saying no to that new idea and you can never experience its true potential as you won't allow the power of the idea to sink in. You will fail to take advantage of the opportunity. Therefore, change before you have to!

Ordinary people strive to maintain status quo when they reach the apex, very rarely will you find someone upsetting the apple cart from such a height. When things go wrong, products fail, teams split, customers retract, revenues tumble, and business goes down, any sane human being would hunt for alternate ways of doing things for survival, but shifting the paradigm when at the helm of success, is the characteristic of a Life Maximizer.

On 15 April, 1955, when Ray Kroc bought the national franchisee of McDonalds from the McDonald Brothers, he was a successful entrepreneur, a wealthy man, living a comfortable life. At 52 he staked his life, career, and fortune and bought McDonalds — an idea that he truly believed in. He pounded the streets of America for several years to make his dream a reality, and never gave up. In the process, he created the fast food industry when nothing of that sort ever existed. He rocked the boat in the middle of the sea with his entire life's earnings and did that at the helm of his career!

Toyota's Qualis was running successfully, selling 8000 units in a single month — the highest ever sales recorded by an SUV.

Toyota then decided to stop the production of Qualis and replace it with Innova.

What if the Innova failed? What if customers didn't buy it? Would they be able to re-introduce Qualis? And what if the Qualis also went out of demand by then? Would they be able to win back the market? Had these been the thoughts running in the mind of the Indian chief of Kirloskar Toyota, they would never have been able to create the thunder that these two products created for Toyota. Well, there was always scope for defeat, scope for failure, a possibility that Innova wouldn't work in the market and by then it would be impossible to revive Qualis as well. But Toyota rocked the boat in the middle of the sea, even as Qualis was at the peak of its success and the result is visible to the world.

All the decisions that each of these individuals/organisations took, were decisions that were well researched, planned and not merely just gut feeling. Had it not been for these bold decisions, risks and challenges, Ray Kroc, Kirloskar Toyota, and thousands like them, would still be running successful entities, flourishing in their personal and professional lives, but the strength of mind and character, self-belief, and the understanding of life they acquired while encountering these experiences would have been missing.

Whether it is changing the structure of your organisation, or launching a new product in an existing or new market; dismissing the top management team because they aren't performing right, or quitting your well paying job to start a new venture; getting married at 29 after many years of bachelorhood or entering a new international market; buying over a company or saying goodbye to your loyal Maruti 800; discontinuing a process or starting a new one… do it when you are at the peak of success, when you have maximum comfort, when you have everything to lose. It's a gamble, play!

I was at the top of my career in corporate training when I rocked the boat and said goodbye to corporate training. I was the darling of the industry. Whether it was Vodafone (then Hutchison Max, Orange), Asian Paints, Coca Cola, or Procter & Gamble, Hindustan Unilever, or Mahindra & Mahindra, Ford, or Hyundai, Standard Chartered Bank, or Sodexo Pass, ITW Signode, or New Holland Tractors, LIC, or Birla Sunlife, Max New York Life, or Metlife, Aviva Life Insurance, or Reliance Life, DLF, or HDFC, ICICI, or Tata Sky, UTI, or Kotak Life, Paras Pharmaceutics, or Saint Gobain, Tata AIG, or Blowplast, Airtel, or HSBC, Ion Exchange, or State Bank of India, SKF Bearing, or Philips, Tata Motors or Sony. Whether it was sales training or leadership, key account management or negotiation skills, change management or people management skills, communication or presentation skills, customer care or quality service... I was the most sought after trainer — well entrenched, well networked, well known, comfortable.

Word of mouth publicity was so strong that I had my entire year booked. I had a full schedule for the next two years and a six-month waiting period. I was at the peak and I said goodbye to the world of corporate training and got into the MSME Sector (Micro, Small and Medium Enterprise). I said goodbye to the glamour of the corporate world and from the world of Coca Cola and Unilever, I came to Spartan Engineering, Shree Ganath Stores, Sai Fasteners, Chinu Travels, Sunny Advertising, Lokesh Jewelers... names only the owner of these companies and their employees knew. These were companies that were not known in the world, not known in India, not known in Maharashtra, not known in Mumbai, not known in Andheri, not known on J. P. Road in Andheri, not known in Akruti Arcade (a building on J. P. Road in Andheri), not known on the fifth floor of the Arcade, not known to the man sitting in Block 504 when you were in Block 506.

I said goodbye to the glamour, the style and pomp of the corporate training world and came down from INR 5000-50,000 crore conglomerates to INR 50 lakh-5 crore companies. I rocked the boat of my life in the middle of the sea. I underwent all the pain and sacrifice, the trials and tribulations of the change and this was not my first change, I have done this 'rocking the boat' several times in the past such that it has now become part of my DNA, my subconscious self, my psyche, my style, my way of life.

I fulfilled all the four conditions of rocking the boat in the middle of the sea:

1. **Believe in the Philosophy of Discontinuity:** I had no problems with discontinuity. I always said goodbye to the comfort and fun of continuity.

2. **Do not ask for a guarantee:** I never asked anybody to guarantee my success, and assure me that everything would be all right. I did not bother wondering if my lifestyle would remain the same, and if I would retain my peace of mind. You would be mad to ask these questions when you are in the middle of the sea. If there was anything that is guaranteed in the middle of the sea, it is death and I continued to rock the boat with death on my side for I always believed that once you die, you don't have to worry anyway, because then it is all over — you can't remember anything, you can't regret. It's fine!

3. **Do not look for endorsements:** I never asked anybody to endorse what I was doing. Whenever you are doing something new, different and better, you are alone. The beauty is your loneliness.

    ► You are bound to look like a fool, accept it

- ► You are bound to be ridiculed, face it
- ► You are bound to be laughed at, allow it
- ► You are bound to be questioned, don't bother about it
- ► You are bound to be in a state of self doubt, remain in it

You are not going to get any endorsements because there is no benchmark against which you can be evaluated. No one has walked on this path. It is not a beaten track, it a track that you are laying. It is in the realm of the unknown that you are stepping. Don't be a fool and ask for an endorsement!

4. **Rock the boat when you are at the peak of success:** I never was afraid about losing my position, so I rocked the boat when I had achieved success. That was when I still had the confidence and time to experiment and make mistakes, go through the pain and the difficulty, much before change was forced on me, much before I had to!

Rocking the boat comes naturally to some people, but others have to strive to make this a part of their psyche. As long as you continue playing within the boundaries of safety and comfort, you will never be able to rock the boat and unless you do that, life maximization will not happen.

In the space below write down how will you rock the boat of life in the middle of the sea, i.e. things that you will discontinue, actions that you will take without the guarantee and endorsement of others and the decisions you will take when you are at the peak of success:

No.	How will you rock the boat in the middle of the sea?	Deadline

Your promise to yourself for this chapter

In order to maximize life for a lifetime, you need to give this order, this instruction, this directive, this mandate, this law of God, this commandment every day, every hour, every minute of your life:

Rock the boat in the middle of the sea.

4

Be autonomous, declare your constitution today

People who are autonomous dare;
and dare you must for Life Maximization.

On 26 January, 1950, exactly three years after India emerged as an independent country, the Drafting Committee of the Indian Constitution chaired by Dr. Babasaheb Ambedkar formed the Constitution of India and laid ground rules for the way it would function as a Democratic Republic — the way it would appoint a Prime Minister, set up the Parliament, hold elections, operate under democratic institutions, and the overall management of an independent country.

The beauty of a constitution is that it gives you a framework within which you can work; it directs your life, not allowing you to collapse. Dr. Babasaheb Ambedkar created one for our country. Dhirubhai Ambani (one of the most highly regarded Indian industrialists) created one for himself. You have to make one for yourself if you want to maximize life!

How many years has it been since you were born, and are you still living without declaring your life's constitution?

To maximize life, be autonomous — declare your constitution today.

I have always believed in the philosophy of 'Fear'. The world must be afraid of you. What I mean is respectful fear. Confused? Respectful fear is the opposite of terrorised fear. When a dacoit, a goon, or a thug places a knife on your neck or points a gun to your head, this elicits terrorised fear, forced fear. This fear can also be created by designations, yelling, shouting at others, or by bullying someone in a position lower than yours.

Respectful fear is private, it is admiration; it is private admiration. It is a way to keep yourself on the top; it is a way to not allow the world to disturb you, bother you or mess with you. It keeps the world at a distance. Respectful fear is a product of autonomy, it is essential, necessary, mandatory, and compulsory for life maximization.

The word autonomous is made up of two terms:

Auto means **Self**
Nomous means **Laws**
Autonomous means **Self Laws.**

Life is an unpredictable game. Everyone has different experiences, and in such a dynamic world, you cannot operate with the rules/laws laid down by someone else. You cannot become a victim of the views and opinions of others. To maximize your potential, you need to be self-created, self-constituted, self-made; you need to be in a state of liberation and confidence. You need to have laws that you have set in place — you need to be autonomous!

Life Maximizers are autonomous individuals. They are not controlled by others or by outside forces; instead, they are self-directed, self-governing, and independent folks who live life on their own terms.

They have laws for everything that they will do and never compromise them. They do not follow norms set by anybody, but themselves. They have a constitution that defines these laws and at periodic intervals they keep making progressive amendments and declare this to the whole world.

For instance, all my customers, colleagues, and friends know I work only on 100% advance payment, which means if someone is hesitant to make the full payment in advance, he or she cannot avail the services of me or my company. I have made myself and my company tough, responsible and capable enough to produce double exemplary results against the investments made by our customers and then influence the world to adhere to it. It is my self-law; I have written it in my constitution of life, communicated it, advertised it, declared it to the world and the world has to abide by it!

The world knows that I am fanatic about being punctual and I don't wait for anybody who comes late. When I was a Branch Manager (head of location) at Eureka Forbes I used to conduct branch meetings for my sales force every Saturday. Our then Managing Director wanted to attend one of my branch meetings. I was India's No. 1 Salesman, No. 1 Group Leader, No. 1 Sales Supervisor and now India's No. 1 Branch Manager. My meetings were known to be fiery, tough and out of the world — full of madness, passion, and inspiration. As the MD of the company, he was intrigued to get a feel of my meetings.

I had an autonomous rule of life — a self-law that all my meetings would start bang on time and in this case it was 1.30 pm. I had informed him about the time and everybody knew that once I commence my meeting, no one including god is permitted into the meeting room. He promised to reach well before time. He was a man of principles and he had always reached on time for all his commitments. That Saturday the entire branch — the accountants, the sales people, customer service team and the security — was on high alert as he was no ordinary person. He was the managing director of the company.

We all got into the room — my 29 sales boys and their leaders. It was close to 1.30 pm at 1.30, I shut the door and started my meeting. He came in at 1.34 pm, saw the door closed, regretted that he could not attend the meeting, privately admired my resolve, privately feared me, and left.

Being autonomous is synonymous with one police officer who during her tenure with the Indian Police Service abided by her self-laws. Kiran Bedi joined the IPS in 1972 and retired in 2007. In those glorious 35 years, she has been the first and the highest ranking Indian woman police officer. She is known for her innovative yet effective approach to law enforcement, which on one hand has helped her achieve extraordinary success in tough environments and on the other hand, been the cause for her frequent and rapid transfers from one department to the other.

She has served in the District Police, Traffic Police, Narcotics Control Bureau, Home Guard, Civil Defence, United Nations Civil Police Advisory, and so on. In each of these stints she has left her audience stunned by her bold and gutsy actions, which also included towing the car of the Prime Minister of India when it was parked in a no-parking zone. Her accolades speak for her self-laws that have always kept her on a higher pedestal compared to the ordinary IPS officers. She was not just an IPS officer, she was an autonomous Life Maximizer.

In one of her assignments as the Inspector General of Prisons, Kiran Bedi revolutionized the very concept of imprisonment taking it upon herself to transform the prisoners of Tihar Jail — a prison with the most dangerous and notorious prisoners ever. Kiran Bedi had a powerful belief that these criminals and murderers who were considered to have no humanity or even sanity left, could also be turned around. She held a ten-day Vipassana (meditation and complete silence camp) course in house — an act that indicated her conviction, daring, and magnanimity.

Where would this campaign be conducted; how could we ensure public safety and control over the prisoners, what if some of them ran out of control and led to an uprising; the infrastructure, the facilities, food, space and hundreds of other things needed to be planned.

There were no patterns for this. No examples. But as it is rightly said, no great successes were created by following set patterns; no conglomerates were built by doing the ordinary; no wars were ever won by doing what was safe and secure and Kiran Bedi was a lady made of self-laws. She believed in doing what was unconventional and she had directed herself to steer this revolution. She created her own patterns. She created her own examples and worked out such a miracle that subsequent generations have wanted to emulate her.

Dhirubhai Ambani was another such man of great self-laws and autonomy. Hailing from a middle-class Gujarati family, he was the son of a village school teacher who started his career as a small time worker with Arab Merchants in Aden in 1950s and from there built the largest private sector company of India — Reliance Industries Ltd. The only law governing his struggle was 'Whatever I will do, will be large, world-class, and first of its kind'. And true to the constitution that he had laid, everything that he did from there — whether it was introducing the stock market to the average Indian investor or setting up one of the world's largest oil refineries in Jamnagar and converting its 'Brass City' image into the 'Oil City of India' bringing a small town like Jamnagar into national and international prominence; investing as much as INR 25,000 crore to introduce optic fibres in Reliance Industries, or building one of the largest conglomerates in the history of this nation — each of these acts was world-class, first of its kind and larger than life. It symbolises speed, excellence, doing the impossible — and these guiding principles of Dhirubhai's life have now become the constitution of Reliance.

Doing things that no one else does requires guts, self-belief, and autonomy of thoughts and actions. Your autonomous behaviour helps the world around you maximize. Respectful fear, a product of being autonomous, exploits the talent in and around you — makes people do what they believed is not possible.

You become the cause of other people's growth; you inspire people to do things that surprises and shocks them. They maximize themselves because you were and are 'autonomous'.

Write down your self-laws

Why are these self-laws essential?

Self-laws provide people with a framework of rules and regulations that directs them towards a righteous code of living. In the absence of this framework, people tend to resort to wrong methodologies such as bribery, betrayal, corruption etc. to reach their goals; they take shortcuts that can lead to adverse consequences in the long run. Several prospective Life Maximizers who could have made it big, fall prey to such negative behaviours. Take for instance, talented cricketers who ruined their career because of their inexplicable involvement in match-fixing or other sportsmen who courted scandal and disgrace. An absence of self-laws killed their maximization.

Be it major ethical issues such as corruption or not paying tax on time, even seemingly smaller offenses such as driving under the influence of liquor, not adhering to traffic rules, etc. if one declares one's constitution and lives by it, life is set on the right track.

In order to maximize life for a lifetime, you need to give this order, this instruction, this directive, this mandate, this law of God, this commandment everyday, every hour, every minute of your life.

Be autonomous, declare your constitution today.

5

Declare that every resource around you will be maximized

The beauty of Life Maximization is that it helps you explore the unexplored inner self of all humans around you.

We live in a technological world; a world where discoveries are being made constantly. However, every new breakthrough undermines a human being's confidence and sense of continuity about his life, future, and existence. Every person's life is becoming increasingly unpredictable. There is turmoil all around us. There is no permanence of income, employment, standard of living, thoughts, strategies, people, loyalty, or life. All over the world, government after government is trying to solve human issues, but they are unable to respond creatively to the never-ending crises created by technology.

Human beings are being treated as depersonalised objects and people are losing sensitivity, love, care and passion for each other. Technological tools, processes, manuals, procedures, software, etc. are being valued more highly than people. That human touch is missing. It is here that growth, creativity, and transformation becomes impossible.

So is technology the culprit? Is technology making us insensitive? Are we losing faith in people and treating them as mere numbers, because we are suffering from technology blindness — a disease that makes us blind to the joy of human relationships? Are we losing interest, contact, and empathy with the people around us? Why are we confused about which culture we should follow — the Indian culture, the American culture, the British culture, the Tamil culture, the Gujarati culture?

A Gujarati boy gets married to a Chinese Muslim girl, goes to America, works there for five years and then settles down in Paris. Should he follow the Gujarati culture or should he follow the Indian culture which is characterised by multiplicity and diversity? Should he follow the Chinese culture or the Muslim culture and that too as it is followed in China? Should he follow the American culture, the Gujarati-American culture, the Gujarati-American-Chinese-Muslim culture, the Gujarati-American-Chinese-Muslim-French-Paris culture? People all over the world get confused with such quandaries.

We live in a new world where all the rules of working, trading, communicating, and living are being challenged and rewritten by the hour. We are losing our grip on our lives and future. It used to be that joint families, communities, religion, and political institutions gave us confidence to explore our own talents, but all these institutions have nearly completely disintegrated. Finding a job is a struggle, but are people sticking to one place? Long-term relationships are rare, countries are collapsing, boundaries are breaking. There is constant disruption of everything around us. Nothing seems to be relevant anymore.

So is this the reality… that we are now more pessimistic than ever before? We are constantly anxious about everything, upset about everything. We are in a maddening rush to achieve everything very quickly, respond very quickly, act very quickly. And if this is the reality, there is another reality that in the middle of all this confusion and uncertainty we have a life and this life has to be maximized. We have goals that have to be achieved; destinations that have to be reached; aspirations that have to be fulfilled; a future that has to be captured. We have human beings around us and they have to be maximized.

'A man wrapped up in himself makes a very small bundle.'

~ Benjamin Franklin

As they say, a single leaf working alone provides no shade. No one can whistle a symphony, it takes a whole orchestra to play it.

You may be a great entrepreneur, but you cannot build an

organisation alone; you may be a brilliant doctor, but cannot put up a hospital alone; you may be a talented architect, but you cannot construct a mansion alone; you may be a passionate social worker, but cannot fight poverty alone; you may be a fervent freedom fighter, but you cannot achieve freedom alone; you may be a committed politician, but you cannot build and transform a nation alone.

To build that great organisation, hospital, mansion, fight poverty, achieve freedom, build a nation, you need supporters, and followers. You need resources to maximize their talent, potential, ambitions, goals, energy, fervour, dedication, and commitment. People may or may not be willing to become Life Maximizers, enthusiasm will have to be injected, success will have to be forced, growth will have to be driven, passion will have to be infused, constraints will have to be challenged, and they will have to be transformed from simple human beings to extraordinary fanatics, from content individuals to ambitious go-getters, from normal folks to abnormal souls, from ordinary mortals to Life Maximizers.

How do we do this? Here, comes the most powerful, progressive and important commandment of the all the eleven:

Declare that every resource around you will be maximized.

I gave myself this commandment 29 years ago — I would maximize every resource around me. Be it my subordinates, colleagues, bosses, customers, the employees of **smm**art, its senior officials, frontline salespeople, my MD, VP, CEOs, driver, watchman, and the girls and boys who run the daily errands. I had decided that every living being in and around me would be maximized.

In the process, I realised that this is not a game for nice, polite, soft-spoken, humble, sensitive, respectful, and courteous human beings, for people are happy the way they are — not wanting to put in more, not wanting to take on challenges, not wanting to grow or make a difference. Or maybe, they want to do all of this, but do not know how or are not willing to pay the price.

If they have to be maximized, they need to become aware of reality. How can they achieve something greater in life, go beyond their imagination, question everything around them? They need to be kicked and cajoled into doing this, and you will have to be ruthless and demanding. Any person's strengths become apparent only when pressurised and pushed to the limit.

I am reminded here of Winston Churchill who said during the World War, 'I have nothing to offer but blood, toil, tears and sweat'. I believe I have been in a state of war for the longest time — a war I declared to take me to the next level and take the people with me to scale greater heights. And like Winston Churchill, I too have no words of love, care, and sympathy to offer, but challenges, hard work and passion. When you become like this, people will either exceed your expectations or break down… there is no third way out. Those who can match your standards of excellence will grow with you, the rest were never meant to be maximizers.

So, inspired by the words of Churchill, 29 years ago I became tough, I became ruthless, I became challenging, hard-hitting, demanding, and I maximized people. I saw this as a mission and became obsessed with the idea of transforming people. Maximizing resources became my national pastime. Every salesman I saw did not seem like a mere salesman anymore; every office assistant I hired went on to become a Branch Manager; every Executive Assistant I worked with was groomed to become the CEO; every VP, CEO, MD was transformed to do bigger and better; every customer was maximized to the fullest. I declared that every resource around me would be maximized — I did it. I continue doing this and will endure till my last breath. I have declared this and there is no going back on my word!

As you read this, what pops up is probably the image of an extremely insensitive human being who has no love, feelings, or respect for people — a tyrant, a dictator, an autocrat — a person who is inhumane, brutal, heartless. But is that what I am, or is that what Life Maximizers are? Is it only toughness and insensitivity that leads to life maximization?

Life Maximizers are quite unreasonable towards the people around them and this strength comes from their affection for people. Life Maximizers love people, they are intoxicated with the idea of transforming people and helping them transcend to greater heights. They believe that every person — whether he/she is desirous or not — has the capacity and the capability to do a thousand times more than what he/she is currently doing, and they take it upon themselves to help people reach that level of maximization.

They know they will be opposed by the same people they are trying to help. Their intent will be questioned, efforts rejected, their actions will be ridiculed. They might even be kicked in the teeth, blamed for ulterior motives, abandoned, betrayed, and taken for granted. And yet they will be unwilling to give up, tone down, express the sensitivity, humanity, and gentleness that is expected from them.

Through all this, people will try to undermine your belief, but derive strength from the Ten Paradoxical Commandments of Leadership introduced by Kent Keith way back in 1968. I have been an ardent follower of these Commandments and was fortunate enough to be exposed to them very early in my life.

Fondly known as 'Anyway Around the World', these 10 Paradoxical Commandments form an essential part of Commandment 5 of Life Maximization:

- People are illogical unreasonable and self-centered; love them anyway.
- If you do good, people will accuse you of selfish ulterior motives; do good anyway.
- If you are more successful than many of your close friends, you will win false friends and true enemies; don't feel bad, succeed anyway.
- The good that you do today, will be forgotten tomorrow; do good anyway.
- Honesty and openness makes you vulnerable and people take advantage of you; be honest anyway.
- The biggest man with the biggest ideas can be shot down by the smallest man with the smallest mind; think big anyway.
- People favour underdogs but follow only top dogs; fight for a few underdogs anyway.
- What you spend years building, may be destroyed overnight; build anyway.
- People really need help, but may attack you if you help them; help them anyway.
- Give the world the best you have and they will kick you in the teeth; give the world the best that you have anyway.

This is what I have learned and know about people!

Your greatest times and greatest memories are going to be about people. The most difficult, frustrating, tragic, hurting times are also going to be about people. These could be the same set of people or not. Remember, in spite of these disappointments and difficulties, when you work with people, build relationships and get them into your world. Keep doing good and for the interest of people, irrespective of what they do to you, because the seed of good will fall one day on a fertile soil and it will germinate into a great tree and these people will bless you financially and professionally and make a difference in your life.

If you have to work on people, you have to love them. And whilst undergoing the MILT course by Aporesh Acharya watching him transform hundreds of people, I learnt the art of loving people by following the '3 As'

A – Accept
A – Adjust
A – Appreciate

If people have to be transformed and maximized, you need to do three things:

1. Accept people as they are
2. Adjust to their idiosyncrasies
3. Appreciate all the good qualities that they bring to the table

Accept

I've always said that life is a package deal and the people around us come in a package. They may have some exceptional qualities and some that may be annoying. They may be genuine, funny, and eccentric at the same time. You cannot like their genuineness and dislike their eccentricity and compartmentalise a person as good, bad, or ugly in your mind based on your likes or dislikes; for if you do that, you will never be able to love them and if you don't love people, you will never be able to maximize them.

If you judge people, you have no time to love them.
~ Mother Teresa

If you have to maximize people, you have to accept them as they are — the whole package — with their good and bad, and work on them.

Adjust

Adjustment is the basis of every relationship. You have to adjust to the idiosyncrasies of people, the traits that you may not like about them, their not-so-very-good qualities, and not get bogged down by their lacunas. Mould your behaviour to work with them and maximize their lives.

Appreciate

This is the most important of the 3As. You will never be able to understand the real beauty of a person unless you appreciate them. You have to appreciate people for the good qualities that they bring to the table and only if you accept and adjust with people, will you be able to appreciate them.

Maximizing yourself

When we talk about maximizing all the resources around you, the greatest resource is you and you have to maximize yourself while maximizing those around you. One of the ways of doing this is by enjoying all that is good about people and drawing inspiration from them to do bigger things in life.

Every person has some good quality — something of value that he/she has to offer to the world. It could be something that you have always observed, admired and maybe envied too; something that you don't have but would love to have; something that is unique about that person. You could be jealous of these special qualities and feel eternally depressed wondering why you don't have it, but this will not get you any closer to acquiring it. Instead, you can enjoy in others what they have and you don't, and the moment your start appreciating this, this quality starts blossoming in yourself and life maximization happens beyond imagination.

I have always enjoyed the charisma of people around me, drew inspiration and learning from them, studied them closely, and replicated their attitudes to maximize my life.

In a career spanning 29 years, I have met millions of people, but there are a few who have left a lasting impact on me because of the great capabilities/qualities/characteristics that they possess. I observed them carefully and imbibed their qualities to become a better human being. Here are a few of the most unforgettable people who have contributed to my growth:

My father had this great capability of reaching anywhere bang on time. I don't remember him ever getting late for an appointment. When I was a child, I started enjoying this habit since it allowed me to study the preparation he made to be on time, and the words he said to others to ensure their punctuality as well. I imbibed this habit making myself a more powerful and commanding human being.

Rajesh Malhotra, one of the finest bosses I've had the pleasure of working with — had innumerable capabilities I picked up very early in life. One such quality that delighted me the most was his ability to manufacture leaders. He empowered people very quickly; he was unafraid of their failure, in fact he inspired young people to take on challenging tasks much before their age and experience would permit, allowed them to make mistakes and then helped them steer out of it. His flagship words were, '*Kuch nahi hota hai...mai baitha hoo naa*' which means, 'Nothing will go wrong, I'm here to handle everything'. And with this few words, he would inspire confidence and courage and people could take on the greatest challenges and emerge triumphant. If someone came to him with a problem, all he would do was talk to them, tell them those inspirational words, and they would go back and solve their problems on their own. I was quick to realise this special capability and '*Kuch nahi hota hai...mai baitha hoo naa*' went on to become my hallmark statement with which I maximized people.

A.W. George, the joint M.D. of Team Productivity and one of my bosses had this great ability to remain calm when challenged in his training programmes and other public forums for his knowledge or lack of it. He handled the situation with grace and humility and this became one of my greatest learnings as a trainer, motivational speaker, and a public figure.

Manish Kaul, another supreme boss in Real Value Appliances (where I sold fire extinguishers) had a fanatic passion for wearing great clothes. Very rarely do I remember seeing him in the same coat more than once. He was impeccably dressed for every interface —

with matching accessories, socks, shoes, ties... His flamboyance, panache, and sense of dressing inspired me to step out of my favourite blacks and blues and have a wider-ranging wardrobe.

Zig Ziglar, one of the world's best known motivational speakers and the supreme authority on sales, has hundreds of books, audios, and videos to his credit and I have been an ardent reader and follower throughout my life. He went across the globe transforming millions and zillions of individuals. I enjoyed his achievements in the field of sales and motivational speeches and that gave me the inspiration to go places and transform people; create over a hundred audio-videos that I have to my credit and maximize my life as a Sales Guru and Motivational Speaker.

Narayan Murthy (of Infosys) and Azim Premji (of Wipro), two of the finest industrialists of India, have always enthralled me with their simplicity, frugality, and humility. Being the multi-billionaires that they are, running huge conglomerates like Infosys and Wipro, I have never seen them splashing money on futile things. They are often seen travelling economy class sitting next to common men, driving simple cars, wearing simple clothes with no flashy watches, gems, or jewels. In spite of being so successful and at the helm of prosperity, they have never allowed success to go to their head and learning this helped me remain grounded regardless of the name, fame, reputation or fan-following that I had.

Surendra Sharma, a renowned Hindi poet and humourist is known for his spontaneity, wit, and style that he brings to each of his acts. He inspired me to create unusual energy, dynamism, and a sense of humour that are today considered to be the USPs of my programmes as a trainer/speaker.

Akhil Marfatia, the former MD of Eureka Forbes, had an innate passion for sales and salespeople and Anil Kumar Gupta (my first boss and the largest contributor to my early professional life) had a zest for teaching sales and helping people accomplish their goals—they made me fall in love with the sales community and help them transcend to greater heights, which I consider my greatest strength in life today.

My Executive Assistant Nausheen, a 23-year-old chirpy girl whose commitment and dedication towards her work is yet another quality that I enjoy. I see mails coming from her at five in the morning, two at night… her hard work, ability to multi-task, take on multiple challenges, unconditional love and loyalty, her passion and the desire to assist me in all my endeavours — all of these rekindle youthfulness and vibrancy in me, making me feel 23 again, thus helping me perform to the best of my abilities.

Dan Sullivan, one of the most celebrated entrepreneur coaches and my mentor in life — introduced hundreds of audios-videos-books on several human subjects that helped me explore the unexplored, know the unknown and venture into unchartered territories. His grip on entrepreneurship helped me understand entrepreneurship better and become an entrepreneurial coach myself. Had I not admired, cherished and enjoyed his creativity and edge, I would not have become what I am today.

Joel Barker, the great American 'Change' Guru's creative ways of presenting his thoughts, views and philosophies on paradigms, leadership and change have been a constant source of inspiration for me, spurring me on to introduce newer subjects and maintain a sense of freshness and originality in each of my programmes.

Verghese Kurien and the work done by him in the arena of dairy development in India has left a lasting impact on me. What did Verghese Kurien have when he left his government job and volunteered to join Shri Tribuvandas Patel, the Chairman of Kaira District Cooperative Milk Producers Union limited (KDCMPUL) to set up a milk processing plant? Did he know that his actions would lead to the birth of Amul — the $2.15 billion dairy co-operative Indian brand? Did he know in 1965 when he was appointed by the then Prime Minister of India, Lal Bahadur Shastri, to create the National Dairy Development Board (NDDB) and replicate the success of Amul throughout India that one day he would be called the 'Father of the Milk Revolution or the White Revolution'? In 1973, when he set up Gujarat Co-operative Milk Marketing Federation (GCMMF) to market the dairy products, did he know that he was making India the largest milk producer in the world, thus becoming the milkman of the nation?

Lee Iacocca and the challenges he undertook to revive Chrysler — the third largest car company in USA — from a state of bankruptcy, immediately after he was humiliated and fired by Henry Ford II of Ford Motors, inspired me to undertake challenges and grow from one level to another.

Martin Luther King, the great American activist had an idea that would transform the lives of millions of black Americans. He fought till he won civil liberties and equality for the blacks. Can I learn a lesson or two about transformation from Martin Luther King? Can I enjoy his ability to transform and accomplish hundreds of my goals by transforming myself and the world? Can I pick up the intensity that he brought to his communication and become a more intense human being? The answer is yes!

My mother Indira Nair and wife Sindhu Nair possess a special ability to be happy at all times. I see Sindhu smiling, enjoying life and content in all circumstances. She is fine with everything around her. She is always happy! This great quality she shares with my mother ensures they are happy through the most difficult, distressing, and derailing situations in life. They inspire me to look at the brighter side of things and enjoy life, for only if I am happy will I be able to maximize my life.

This list can go on and on. I enjoyed the capabilities/qualities/characteristics of all these influential leaders and many other bosses, subordinates, and colleagues I worked with. I enjoyed their strengths and instead of being displeased with their weaknesses I maximized life for myself and the world.

We all come across people from whom we can learn something or the other. It could be someone's dedication, honesty, creativity, commitment, intelligence, willpower, spontaneity, the ability to love unconditionally, care, give away knowledge for free, stand for what they feel is right. Someone may have mastered a language, have a great sense of humour or sarcasm, ability to connect with people of varied backgrounds, while others may be determined to fight for a cause, be concerned about social service and philanthropy. A life maximizer has to be extremely observant and alert about what people bring to the table, identify behaviour patterns and as your subconscious mind makes a note of it, the same qualities become part of you. One day you will realise that you have changed, you are someone you always wanted to be.

So when you see someone with great qualities/capabilities, don't be upset or jealous. Acknowledge them, appreciate them, enjoy learning from them and allow it to happen to yourself as well.

In the table given on the following page, make a list of at least ten people who have impacted your life, list the greatest capabilities / qualities / characteristics you enjoy in them and construct a game plan for how you will bring them into your life. This could be through reading, audio-videos, keen observation, appointing a coach/advisor, undergoing a training programme, etc.

In order to maximize life for a lifetime, you need to be conscious of this order, this instruction, this directive, this mandate, this law of God, this commandment every day, every hour, every minute of your life:

Declare that every resource around you will be maximized

No.	Decisions	Capabilities/qualities/ characteristics you enjoy	How will you bring it into your personality?
1			
2			
3			
4			
5			
6			
7			
8			
9			
10			

6

Declare your thoughts, words, and deeds

Most actions of people are circumstantial. Be careful.

During the very early days of my career, when I was working in India's greatest direct sales company Eureka Forbes, I was gifted a Signature wrist watch signed by the legendary J.R.D. Tata (Chairman of Tata Group from 1932-1992, i.e. 60 years). The watch had three words inscribed on it: 'Humata Hukhta Huvarshta'. I asked the senior management to explain what those words meant, because if Mr. Tata had autographed it, those words must have a deep meaning. I was told it meant, 'Good Thoughts, Good Words, Good Deeds'.

J.R.D. Tata built India's best managed, most reputed, and trusted industrial house, and even today it is a world leader. He had maximized life. I knew why. The answer lay in these three words, 'Good Thoughts, Good Words, Good Deeds'. At that tender age, inspired by the philosophies of this legendary man, I declared that I would throughout my life be dictated by this philosophy!

People have a lot of dreams and ambitions in life. They want to enjoy the best luxuries, achieve higher ranks, travel the world, expand their business, enter new markets, and fulfill their career aspirations. They may have dreams for their families — giving the best education to their kids, providing the best life to their parents, and so on. But life is unpredictable, evolving, and full of surprises, always demanding more than what you can offer. It is never easy, simple, or straight.

You may have decided to complete your six-month long assignment in three months and return home. But just as you give the assignment the final touches, you meet with an accident and are advised four months of complete bed rest.

You may have worked very hard to bag a project and just when it was supposed to be given to you, your boss's first cousin enters the business and bags it as his pilot.

You may be all geared up for the long holiday that you have

planned with your wife and kids after almost a decade, and the day you're supposed to leave, you're asked to report to work to handle an unforeseen emergency.

You may have waited for months for your dream project and the day you get it, your twelve-year old daughter is diagnosed with cancer.

Today, businesses are shutting down faster than they are launched, people are losing jobs by the hour, resignations are given at the drop of a hat, business deals are lost, promotions are declined, relationships are breaking at lightning speed, and stress levels are zooming up.

During such challenging times, people tend to lose their sense and sensibilities and start sensationalising their situations. They cannot think objectively, their communication pattern becomes one of a disturbed, depressed, defeated human being, and their actions depict the loss of love, passion and zest for life. They forget their goals and are crippled by the difficulties of their present circumstances, and develop thoughts, words, and deeds that drown them in the ocean of self-defeat.

These thoughts, words and deeds are often influenced by one's situation. As long as everything is smooth, one may be positive, and ready to take on challenges, but if untoward events occur, their positivity instantly turns into negativity, they lose their love and passion for life, their determination and inspiration goes down and they hide in their own shell. They start complaining instead of creating, compromise instead of confront, accept instead of question, and give up instead of fight back. They act without thinking it through, and it is possible they will regret this.

One of my colleagues at **smm**art was a woman named Smitha who earlier ran a playschool for kids in Mumbai. Way back in 1998, when the playschool business was not as famous and popular as it is today, she had a well established setup with two classrooms, 34 students, and four teachers on her payrolL She had been successfully running the business for seven years. The giants in the business, Kangaroo Kids had offered her franchisee opportunities and she was very enthusiastic and ambitious about taking her small dream beyond the confines of her home and vicinity.

In the seventh year of her business, she lost her mother-in-law and the responsibilities of taking care of the home, her father-in-law, and her son who was just three years old then, rested on her shoulders. She believed that now her priority was home, her father-in-law, and her child. Nothing in life mattered more than this. As I said, most actions are circumstantial, she sensationalised her situation beyond what it really was and in a fraction of a moment, decided to shut shop, take a sabbatical and focus on the home front, prioritising her domestic duties.

In just four months, her father-in-law had settled in his new routine, her son got involved in his pre-school and she once again had the opportunity to focus on her career. She then took up a job as a teacher in a school and moved on in life, but till today she regrets her overnight decision to shut down the playschool.

That business that could have become the Kangaroo Kids, Tree House, and EuroKids of today (some of the most famous playschools in India). But she fell prey to circumstances and the emotional turmoil that resulted from these circumstances and sacrificed her dreams. And the extent of human ignorance is so huge that this did not even occur to her till I happened to have a conversation with her about this, when she connected the dots and realised the entire game that circumstances play on our thoughts, words, and actions.

People get emotionally paralysed by their circumstances and allow their sentiments to dictate their actions. Think about this,

99% of the population takes decisions based on their emotions and circumstances. If you doubt this, look at the decisions people around you have taken in the last three months and you will be convinced!

People quit jobs because a promotion is declined, shut down business because of a bad month/quarter, get depressed because of a relationship breakdown, give up on life because of a family tragedy, etc. A decision taken during a state of mental, emotional, and psychological helplessness is thoughtless, shortsighted, destructive, and detrimental to Life Maximization.

As Epictetus once said, 'Situations in this world do not disturb us, it is our view of them that disturbs us.' I have seen hundreds and thousands of people lose out in life because of their circumstantial thoughts, words, and deeds and the emotional decisions that need to be taken then, which only takes them farther and farther from their goals and ambitions.

And as I saw people losing out on life because of this, I realised that these are the people who have not understood that life will play tricks all the time, and to give up during such a phase is effortless — it does not require any special pains. But amidst all this chaos and ups and downs, to keep yourself aligned to your goals and not let the unpredictability of life overpower your objective is the hallmark of a true Life Maximizer. Your goals may get delayed, but you have to continue pursuing them and this requires confidence. The definition of confidence, as understood by me is:

Confidence is an eternal (lifetime) ability to remain composed, alert, and directed in your thoughts, words, and deeds when faced with the fears and insecurities that surround us.

(Read this definition several times before you proceed)

Not that such events do not occur in the life of Life Maximizers — they too lose business, deal with resignations, suffer from relationship breakdowns, encounter death in the family and other tragedies of life. But they have instructed themselves — commanded, ordered, demanded — that they will remain composed, alert, and steady in their thoughts, words, and deeds under all circumstances.

Zig Ziglar, one of the greatest motivational speakers once said, 'Your language, your vocabulary will become your actions.' How true! Most people are unable to think the right thoughts, words, and deeds. Many are directed by someone else's thoughts, words, and deeds. The problem lies with their language!

I realised that I had a fan following in every party, social gathering, or corporate congregation I attended. I was quite a star wherever I went. People wanted to meet me, share a few words, ask a question, as if I had answers to all their problems. I realised why. In my language, there was enthusiasm, the spirit of a fighter, the strength to question the status quo, guts, and possibilities to do the unknown, no complaints, no remorse, no regret. There was a certain motivation, optimism, courage, and progression… there was no regression!

Many years ago, I had looked into the *Oxford Dictionary* to know what 'progression' meant and as I understood the meaning of it, I embedded it in my psyche.

Progression: A gradual movement or development towards a destination or a more advanced state. A number of things coming one after the other.

When I looked at both definitions, I manipulated it to my advantage — that's the beauty of a Life Maximizer. He is an opportunist. He can pick up anything from anywhere to suit his requirement and stay maximized!

For me the second part of the definition, i.e. 'A number of things coming one after the other' meant a number of resignations one after the other, a number of breakdowns one after the other, a number of debacles one after the other, and a number of problems, personal and professional, occurring one after the other.

For instance,

➜ *Your wife suffers a miscarriage today*

➜ *You lose your job tomorrow*

➜ *Your partner starts a similar business without your permission and siphons off money from your business*

➜ *Death of a loved one*

➜ *A serious illness*

➜ *Your father telling you to quit your job and come home every day before 7 pm and your job at the age of 23 is generally expected to finish by 10 pm*

➜ *Your husband asking you to quit your job because he cannot take how famous you are in the company*

➜ *Your loved one being raped*

➜ *A union being formed by your workers*

➜ *A factory being forced to shut down*

➜ *A fraud in your company*

➜ *You being wrongly framed in a legal dispute*

➜ *The promotion that you don't get even though you were the best*

- → *Four of your top achievers resigning together without serving their notice period*
- → *Giving birth to a differently-abled child*
- → *Your child fails in the most important exam of his life*

You may be rejected by people, promises may be broken, commitments are forgotten… my dear friends it could be anything in business, job, or life.

You have no control over such problems and you are not responsible for any of them, but when it happens, it could happen at any time.

Any or all of these problems can occur in life as per the second definition of progression. Either I or someone close to me has faced one or some of these problems. But, the directive I gave myself many, many years ago was, 'Santosh Nair, when you encounter any or all of these incidents that can derail you, you will be aware, alert, and steady in your thoughts, words, and deeds. You will never think regressively, your language will not be that of a loser and you will never act like one. Your life is not a wooden plank floating on the ocean, your life is a ship with a rudder. And your rudder will navigate the ship in the direction you want. You will face any or all of these situations in life, but your thoughts, words, and deeds will be progressive — that will move you forward.'

This is where I come to the first definition of progression. I realised that irrespective of the problem, I will gradually move forward; I will move towards my desired destination and convey my thoughts, words, and deeds such that I will reach that desired destination I want in my life.

It therefore becomes clear to you that Life Maximizers at any given point in time have clear destinations to reach, clear goals and targets to achieve, and a clear purpose to accomplish. And they know while they are moving towards their purpose a number of things will happen one after the other without their permission/will, and the only thing that will help them progress is their language, their vocabulary, their state of mind which will direct their thoughts, words, and actions.

And so, I declared that whatever be the situation, and state of my mind, I will move forward towards my destination. I will favour and pursue new, different, and better ideas and not be cowed down by the status quo that life wants me to maintain. I will not take decisions while in a broken state, that will lead to regression. I will face all challenges, head on. I will undergo the pain and agony of the present difficulties for I know that, this state, this difficult state will soon pass. I am ready for the physical, mental, emotional, and psychological pain. I am ready, I am ready, I am ready to fight a prolonged battle of life. I will fight, I will achieve, I will conquer! Yes, I know that I will never be in a position to control events in my life; however, I can and I will definitely control my thoughts, words, and deeds!

On 10 March, 1981, Morris E. Goodman — a successful American businessman and a pilot by passion — left his home on a pleasure trip in his own airplane. It crashed. His survival became medical history. After seeing him being brought into the hospital, the doctor rushed to Goodman's wife and said, 'Mrs. Goodman I have been in the medical profession for a good number of years and the fact that your husband is still alive will itself make medical history. No man to my knowledge has ever survived a break in his neck. Your husband's neck is broken at two places. His spinal cord is almost crushed. His neck is damaged so severely that he will never be able to speak again. He is suffering permanent nerve damage leading to dysfunctional liver, bladder, kidneys, and diaphragm which means he will never be able to breathe without the use of a respirator. His swallowing reflexes are damaged so severely that he won't be able to eat or drink again. I'm sorry to have to tell you all this but quite candidly I don't think he will survive the night.'

Everybody had decided that Morris would not survive, except one person — Morris himself. He could not even nod his head and was asked to indicate with the blink of his eye, if he wanted to undergo a life saving one-of-its-kind surgery which had a strike rate of 1:1000 with an understanding that even if he were to survive, the best that could happen to him was to be able to sit in a wheelchair, 20-odd months from now, for the rest of his life and that too would be a miracle.

With just a blink of his eye, Morris did not only give his consent to undergo the surgery but also set a goal for himself that he would survive the operation and walk out of the hospital on his own two feet before Christmas 1981. His thoughts, his words and his deeds were those of a Life Maximizer!

He was operated and since the surgery was a success, the doctors declared he had slim chances of survival. But they explained, Morris would never be able talk, move, or breathe on his own, without a respirator, ever again in life. The doctors left him with the impression that he would be nothing more than a vegetable for the rest of his life, but that was not the picture he saw of himself. He believed with all his heart and mind that he would be normal soon and when he closed his eyes he could see himself flying his most beloved aircraft again.

With positivity in his thoughts, words, and deeds, he set short-term and long-term goals for himself — the long-term goal of walking out of the hospital on his own two feet before Christmas that year and the short-term goal of being able to speak, breathe without the machine, swallow food, and then walk out of the hospital.

He devised ways of communicating with the hospital staff with the use of charts and images and his next task was to breathe independently. Each time he tried to do that all he faced was failure but unwilling to give up, he persisted. When he was being shifted to another hospital, with the use of charts and images — his preferred method of communication — he left a message for the doctor who had operated on him:

'Please tell Dr. Matthews that in the next six months, I'll be back to this hospital and when I come back, I will walk into his office and shake his hand.'

The hospital staff thought Morris was a fool for believing he could achieve his goal and the genuine ones — those who empathised with him — told him that it would be a lot easier for him to accept that this would not be not possible rather than torturing himself with such impossible dreams. But Morris knew he would make it happen. And true to his belief, he did walk out of the hospital on his own two feet before Christmas day that year. What drove him were his thoughts, words, and deeds:

Thoughts: His thoughts were those of a fighter. He truly believed that he would survive and emerge from this tragic incident as normal as he had been through life.

Words: His words were that of revival. With just the blink of an eye, he had communicated that he was going to be fine, to himself as well as to the doctors. He kept telling his wife, his sister, his visitors and the hospital staff that he would be fine soon and they would all see him walk out of the hospital hale and hearty.

Deeds: All his deeds were that of a survivor. He would keep a ball on his throat and try speaking for endless hours, not getting tired, not giving up. Going against the hospital rules and regulations, he would call for outside food and try to swallow juice. He would practise walking in spite of a few accidents while doing so. He listened to the motivational audios of Zig Ziglar that nurtured hope and optimism, reminding him of his goals and the power of his goals, thus infusing faith in the belief that he could achieve what he wanted.

He rekindled hope in co-patients who were declared to be handicapped as well, that if he could recover from such a near-death accident and dare to become normal again, they too could overcome their physical disabilities and look forward to a normal life, irrespective of what medical science indicated, thus becoming a source of strength and courage for several people.

Everybody around him knew that one day he would achieve what he had decided for himself and they all got together to garner his dream, helping him in his journey, in whatever way possible. Not only did he walk out of the hospital on his own two feet on the date he had declared and start living a normal life very soon after that, but Morris left a lasting impact on all those he encountered during this period, which is why he is fondly called the 'Miracle Man' across the globe!

Let us further examine the importance of thoughts, words, and deeds and how they can make or break our life, through the story of another legendary man. During World War II, millions of Jews, Poles, Russians, and Gypsies were rounded up by the Germans and mercilessly put to death. This period was known as the Holocaust — the genocide of European Jews and others by the Nazi Government. Amongst the millions who became victims of this brutal practice was a man called Victor Frankl. Victor was a psychiatrist from Vienna. He had a successful practice, lived a good life, but was a Jewish and owing to this, he was deported to one of these Nazi concentration camps called Auschwitz to be executed. When he arrived there and witnessed the carnage, Victor set three goals for himself:

1. To survive

2. To use his medical skills and help those he could

3. To try and learn something amidst this Holocaust (a goal only a Life Maximizer could have set for himself while ordinary mortals were preparing themselves mentally, emotionally and psychologically to embrace death)

Victor truly did achieve all three goals. He came to be known as a Holocaust Survivor and later the author of the bestseller *Man's Search for Meaning* in which he shared his experience in the concentration camps and illuminated all that he learnt from that hell on earth.

In his book, Frankl said that most of the prisoners who entered Auschwitz with him were executed as soon as they arrived. But he had made up his mind that he would survive and with the sheer strength of his thoughts, words, and deeds, he achieved his first goal, which was to escape immediate death — unlike the majority — and be nominated as one of those who were put to work in those horrible conditions.

Whilst at Auschwitz, Victor went through the most difficult period of his life. In spite of all the optimism, positivity, and determination that he had, it is only natural for a man to lose his sense and sensibilities when exposed to such horrid circumstances and Victor was no exception. Sitting alone in a dark room, endlessly waiting for the next bizarre thing to happen, trifling thoughts crossed his mind — would he get food to eat at night, should he exchange a piece of sausage for a piece of bread, should he trade his cigarette for a bowl of soup, and so on.

But he had declared that he would always be a Life Maximizer and he forced his thoughts to another subject. Suddenly he saw himself standing on the platform of a well-lit lecture room in Vienna addressing an audience that was attentive and intrigued. He was happy, free from all sufferings, living an independent life once again. He was giving a lecture on the Psychology of the Concentration Camp. He said to himself that he would make this vision come true and stepped on to a difficult path to make it happen.

His thoughts, words, and deeds were that of a man who was going to survive hell. He succeeded in rising above the situation and conquering the suffering, this gave him the courage, patience, and perseverance to fight this battle until he had accomplished all the three goals that he had set for himself.

The greatest lesson that I learnt from both these legends many years ago, was that if someone like Goodman and Frankl can escape from the jaws of death by the sheer strength of their thoughts, words, and deeds, we, who are not even anywhere close to the vegetative state that Morris was in or the inhumane, helpless conditions that Victor Frankl experienced, we could achieve so much for ourselves and the people around us, making this world a better place. And yet, we spend our lives complaining about the petty things around us, cribbing, and crying about trivial matters and end up being ordinary mortals.

Thoughts, words and deeds, my dear friends, have a huge role to play in deciding the way in which we mould our lives and hence my strong advice to everyone is that your thoughts, words, and deeds should be watched carefully and shaped such that you leave behind the ordinary things and work towards Life Maximization.

Way back in 1989, when I was the Head of Location at Eureka

Forbes, my goal in life was to become the Divisional Sales Manager. During those days, three of my immediate bosses wanted me to take a transfer to Gujarat. I was preparing for my Masters of Marketing Management (MMM) degree from the Narsee Monjee Institute (part-time 7-9 pm) and hence did not want to take that transfer. My bosses were quite upset and since I did not agree to take the transfer, the promotion to the position of Divisional Sales Manager was given to one of my colleagues. I was India's No. 1 Branch Manager, the most deserving candidate with the highest sales figures and yet the promotion did not come to me. The No. 2 Branch Manager was given the opportunity to take over and not only that, he was also made my boss. For an egoistic person, this could be a moment of humiliation and disgrace, for a Life Maximizer it was an event, which could be won back over a period of time. This was a very delicate moment in my life and shattered by this injustice, I could have lost all hope and faith in Eureka (regressive thought), cried and cribbed about all the wrongs done to me (regressive words) and quit (regressive deed).

All my colleagues, subordinates and friends, angry with this unfair act wanted to stand up for me and fight against the management. They told me to revolt against this decision and assured me of their support. Branch Managers of other locations instigated me to protest. There were genuine people who sympathised with me and then there were some who wanted to ride on my wave, and fulfill their own vested interests. I was extremely alert to this politics and games that people play and refused to fall prey to any such ulterior motives. Again, I had the ambition of becoming the boss of these people and was very careful to not expose any weak thoughts, words, or deeds that would hold me morally obligated to reciprocate this help and support if a similar situation occurred with any of them in the future.

So what did I do? I was directed by the goals that I had set for myself and the position I wanted to reach sooner or later and did not allow any of this to manipulate me. There could have been two approaches that I could have adopted — first, I know what happened with me was wrong and I felt terrible about it. I was as angry as my colleagues, or maybe more, but I suppressed my negative emotions and kept myself charged and steady; geared up to stage an even more powerful comeback that would force the management to revoke its decision and later at an appropriate moment take an eye for an eye. In the second way, the injustice I went through did not even register and without any malice or revenge in mind, I set out to conquer bigger milestones.

The former approach was that of intelligence and the latter of wisdom. I chose to be wise!

I did not allow negative emotions to overwhelm me for even a nanosecond and thoughts of taking revenge or revolting never even occurred to me because I had instructed myself many years ago that I would be unmoved by such incidents. I remained as motivated, committed, and directed as I always was, for my focus was still on my goal of becoming the Divisional Sales Manager. In fact I doubled my performance from the very next day and started working more rigorously towards my target. The management took notice of this, understood the plot, and led me to my goal. For me, moving forward is what mattered the most and I did not allow my progress to be wrecked by circumstances or emotions.

I believed in what Henry Ford said, 'If you think, you can; or if you think you can't, either way you are right.' As a salesperson, if you go to the field thinking that your sale will not happen, you will certainly come back empty handed. If you begin negotiations believing that you will not be able to bring down the price to what you want, your opponent will get his price. If you are convinced that your facility can only produce 500 tonnes and not more, you will never be able to even gun for 750. As you believe, so it happens! Your thoughts determine your victory or defeat and if Life Maximization has to happen, you have to win on an hourly basis because the accumulated experience of winning is very important. Therefore, all your thoughts, words, and deeds should be in the direction of winning.

Make a list of all the worst things that could happen to your life 20, 30, 40, 50 years down the line — things related to your family, friends, career, future, business, relationships, health, and so on.

Declare how your thoughts, words, and deeds will be when faced with any or all of the above tragedies and how you will remain focused and move ahead:

____

____

____

____

____

____

____

____

____

____

____

____

____

____

____

____

____

There have been times when I have been completely disillusioned, dejected, and shaken from within and such times come to me as often as they may come to anybody else, but I never allow these moments of depression to remain for longer than a few seconds, minutes, or hours, let alone weeks and months.

I was very quick to realise that when you are depressed, demotivated, and shattered, there is only one person who can pull you out of this state and that is you, yourself. So when you know that you and only you have to pull yourself out of depression, my question is, 'Why do you go into it in the first place?' Thus, to remain motivated and in the best spirits constantly, for a lifetime, one has to develop a mechanism — a support system that will help make this process simple.

This mechanism comprises the following three elements:

1. People
2. Books, Audios, Videos
3. Connecting with the Past

People

I carved out my support system from the people around me. I identified a selected few people in my life — my mother who has been my greatest motivator in life, my wife Sindhu, my Executive Assistant Nausheen and some close colleagues and friends — and designated them as my CMOs (Chief Motivating Officers). I declared that I would only go to them when I am disillusioned, dejected, and shaken, for I know that their belief in me is stronger than my own belief in myself and they would transform my depression, demotivation, and dejection into instant inspiration, optimism, and resolve. This will enable me to look at life with new energy, enthusiasm, and confidence, reinforcing positivity and progressiveness in my thoughts, words and deeds.

Books, Audios, Videos

I sought further solace in the books, audios and videos that have formed my thoughts, words and deeds during the early days of my career. *The Achievement Challenge* by Don Beverage, *The 7 Spiritual Laws of Success* by Deepak Chopra, Jonathan *Livingston Seagull* and *Illusions* by Richard Bach are some of the books that till date remain my permanent source of inspiration and optimism. Whenever low or unhappy with myself, I surrender myself into the arms of these books to show me the way forward and I have yet to experience an occasion when these books have not been able to give me a solution to my problem.

Connecting with the past

My last and the ultimate motivating mechanism remains connecting with my past by going to places which marked the greatest struggles, transformation, and successes in the early days of my professional life. When emotionally low, I often go to Sukanya, a frugal bar in Andheri east (Mumbai) where I would sit and drink after a long and exhausting day on the field as a sales manager; Khushro Baug, in Parsi Colony, where I sold the maximum number of vacuum cleaners while at Eureka Forbes. I travel in a local train, or bus, or walk down the street from Proctor Road to Slater Road in Grant Road east that used to be my sales territory once upon a time, or from Dhake Colony to Andheri station that I would walk every day to save 40 paise.

Each of these places takes me back to where I started off from as a debt-ridden door-to-door salesman of Eureka Forbes; and while sipping a drink at Sukanya I look at my life — a reasonably lavish home, the S-Class Mercedes standing outside, the luxuries and riches of life, smmart, the millions of lives transformed and the respect and reputation earned — the realisation of having made it fairly big in life from there to where I stand today, infuses the courage, belief, and confidence in me that the way forward isn't any different.

Left alone in today's world, one can lose enthusiasm for life, develop negative thoughts, words, and deeds and make destructive decisions that can derange life completely. But to maximize life, you have to create support systems and mechanisms around you that ensure that you remain positive, and progressive, through the most frustrating situations.

Your CMOs (Chief Motivating Officers), books, audio, videos and means of connecting with the past may be vastly different form mine, so I am not recommending any book, or audio or video that will serve as your mechanism. Develop your own support system that pulls you out of momentary dejection and miseries.

List your CMOs, books, audio, videos and means of connecting with the past that you will use to remain motivated and inspired in your thoughts, words, and deeds.

CMOs:

____

____

____

____

____

____

____

____

____

____

Books, Audios, Videos:

Connecting with the past:

You have to give yourself a commandment to remind you to exercise this mechanism when you are discouraged. And yet your mind will play its tricks, keeping you away from these means but the strength of your commandment has to be such that it can rise above such hurdles.

You cannot give this commandment when you are already going through a challenging phase in life. You have to give it today and keep reminding yourself of it every day so you can remain committed when faced with the fears and insecurities that surround us.

I gave myself this commandment on 4 October 1985, when I started my career with Eureka Forbes. I followed these principles when I was 19, 29, 39, 45, and at 49 today, I am all excited and energised to fight any challenge that life can throw at me and all set to conquer the world around.

In order to maximize life for a lifetime, you need to give this order, this instruction, this directive, this mandate, this law of God, this commandment everyday, every hour, every minute of your life. The sixth of the eleven commandments:

Declare your thoughts, words, and deeds.

7

Declare to be a leader for life

Purposeless living impacts no one.

As I said at the beginning of this book, this book is not for ordinary mortals who live ordinary lives under ordinary circumstances. It is for those who have the courage and the guts to do the extraordinary and in the process of doing so, defy the status quo, break accepted norms, fight their personal and professional challenges and build their name, fame, and reputation such that they leave a lasting impression on the world that will take notice of their visit to this planet. This species of people are known as 'Leaders'.

As Joel Barker says,

'A leader is a person you choose to follow to a place where you wouldn't go by yourself.'

Read this definition a minimum of four times before proceeding.

This is no ordinary statement made by an ordinary thinker or philosopher. It is a very profound definition expressed by one of the greatest authorities on Leadership, Joel Barker. A definition which if understood well and ingrained can become the greatest 'Guru Mantras' on leadership ever. And for the benefit of everyone, let me repeat it,

'A leader is a person you choose to follow to a place where you wouldn't go by yourself.'

Any thoughts about which place you wouldn't dare go by yourself? The most common answer is 'the future'.

The next question then is, 'Why wouldn't you go by yourself to the future?' Let me also answer this for you — the future is scary, it is the unknown and is untested. It is daunting, creepy and terrifying, full of uncertainty and insecurity, full of risks and fear. The future could also mean death or complete devastation. This no ordinary game, and for people to achieve extraordinariness in life, to reach those aspirations and ambitions that they can envision but cannot achieve alone, they need a leader — a person that they will choose to follow and the word 'choose' here makes all the difference.

I see a lot of people — leaders, so to say — upset and angry with their subordinates for not listening to their instructions or not following their command, failing to realise that it is not in the hands of the leader to impress upon the follower to follow him/her, but it is purely the choice of a follower whether or not to follow a person whom he considers to be a leader. And hence, in order to maximize your life, you have to declare that you will be a leader for life.

And in order to be the leader that people will choose to follow, you will have to develop special capabilities, capacities, and qualities that influence people around you to follow you; you will have to build a character so strong that people would want to be with you; you will have to develop a language that is so contagious that people would want to emulate you. Extraordinary leadership characteristics will have to be demonstrated.

One cannot become a leader by coincidence. It will have to be planned. This is not a one-time decision, but a lifetime declaration that shall change only with your passage and to do so, you will have to declare today, at 26, 35, 43 — or whatever your age may be — that you will be a leader for life and willing to sacrifice all that comes in the way of this responsibility!

I had made such a decision way back in 1985 when I started my career at Eureka Forbes and let me tell you about the declaration I made to that effect in 1992 when I met Sindhu, my wife-to-be. Much before we got married, during our early engagement days, I remember telling her, 'Sindhu, you are not getting married to an ordinary man. I am a leader and my life is dedicated to the cause of transforming people. Do not expect me to come back home at 5.30 pm like ordinary husbands, take you out for movies and dinners on the weekends, and be next to you whenever you are unwell. You will only get as much time in my life as any other human being would, for I have a cause to fulfill, a mission to achieve, a world to change and that will always remain my priority.'

And since then till today, I have worked like a leader, behaved like a leader, lived like a leader and a leader I shall remain till my last breath.

Leaders can also be defined as, **'Individuals who direct the ordinary folk in all areas of life — personal, professional, and spiritual — thereby challenging accepted norms, philosophies, rituals, cultures and set patterns of society.'**

As I write the above definition and read every word of it, I am reminded of a lady who exemplifies every word of this definition; in fact it wouldn't be incorrect for me to say that her life has inspired me to write this thought-provoking definition.

The winner of several prestigious awards and accolades, Madam Curie was the first woman to win a Nobel Prize, the only woman to win it in two different fields, and the only person till date to win in multiple sciences (Physics and Chemistry). Being deprived of higher education in her homeland Poland due to her gender, Curie challenged accepted norms, philosophies, rituals, and set patterns of society and moved to Paris to pursue her interests in Physics, Chemistry, and Mathematics.

Along with her husband Pierre Curie, she faced several personal and professional setbacks and downfalls, but she continued her research in natural sciences for years to give the world the gift of two key radioactive discoveries 'Polonium' and 'Radium.' In her short stint on this planet, she presented 'radiation' as a means by which cancer could be successfully treated, thus introducing a possible cure in the early stages of cancer.

Unaware of the damaging effects of ionizing radiation back then and even unbothered to find out about it; she continued her research work in open sheds without any safety measures. She carried test tubes containing radioactive isotopes in her pocket and stored them in her desk drawer as if they were ordinary particles, but never allowed the risk of this illness or the fear of death to stop her and in the process she herself fell prey to a disease known as Aplastic Anemia caused by her long-term exposure to radiation and passed away at the age of 66, leaving behind a legacy that is cherished till today.

So high was the level of the radioactivity under which she operated and so fatal was its impact that her research papers from the 1890s are still kept in lead-lined boxes, and those who wish to consult them wear protective clothing before coming in direct contact with it, but none of these safety measures ever occurred to Madam Curie while she was on her quest to discover radioactivity — to give this world something that would make it a better place for those who were to come years after her death.

Such is the intensity, dedication, and commitment of leaders that life itself seems unimportant while they pursue their cause.

She was truly a leader and the world chose to follow her for as long as she lived on this planet. Millions of ordinary mortals have been born and died since she made her discovery, and they didn't even make their presence felt on those around them.

What distinguishes leaders from ordinary mortals is what they decide to do with this one life, and that is what makes them unforgettable. They also experience numerous setbacks and failures, but they do not allow these disappointments to stop them. They are firm believers of the most important quality of a leader:

Fail Fast to Succeed Sooner!

The beauty of leaders is that they are ready to take on challenges that ordinary mortals would not even dare to and are willing to be tested in their area of personal and professional performance and then use that success and failure to go to the next level by improving on their failures and successes. They are willing to be tested, measured, and laughed at and are unafraid of the truth that will emerge when they are judged by the world. They are willing to be ridiculed, exposed as weak, incompetent, ambitious idiots and yet pursue their cause of creation, their cause of excellence. They are ready to accept defeat and start all over again. They are unafraid of losing their present status for their cause, their security, their self image and that is how they become leaders... Life Maximizers!

Take a look at these series of events:

1831 - Lost his job

1832 - Defeated in the run for Illinois State Legislature

1833 - Failed in business

1834 - Elected to Illinois State Legislature

1835 - Sweetheart died

1836 - Had nervous breakdown

1838 - Defeated in run for Illinois House Speaker

1843 - Defeated in run for nomination to U.S. Congress

1846 - Elected to Congress

1848 - Lost re-nomination

1849 - Rejected for land officer position

1854 - Defeated in run for U.S. Senate

1856 - Defeated in run for nomination for Vice President

1858 - Again defeated in run for U.S. Senate

1860 - Elected President of United States of America

(By Ron Kurtus, Founder of the School for Champions educational and personal development website)

This is the story of Abraham Lincoln, one of the most successful and cherished Presidents of the United States of America and the first one from the Republican Party. Lincoln never feared failures; in fact his life is a series of failures, which transformed him into a person who turned these failures into stepping stones for future success.

Let's come to the corporate world now, which has been an ocean of failures and successes. Known today as a business magnate, philanthropist, and social entrepreneur, Henry Ford actually failed several times in his life:

➔ When he first started Detroit Automobile Company, his first group of investors withdrew after Ford had spent $86,000 without producing a car that could be sold

➔ He eventually produced a car and raised another $60,000 in share capital, but Detroit Automobile Company went bankrupt in 1901, because of 'customer complaints of high prices and low quality'

➔ The second company that he started, Henry Ford Company, collapsed due to a fight with a partner

- In the late 1920s, Henry Ford refused to update the Model T car or bring out any newer models, leading his third company, Ford Motor Company, to collapse because of low sales
- Ford tried to launch a political career, but never succeeded
- He failed and went broke five times in his entrepreneurial journey

And yet it was the same Henry Ford who is known to have revolutionised car engineering, assembly line production, business, social leadership in business, education, and other areas. And the Ford Motor Company that he started way back in 1903 and built, overcoming hundreds of failures, is the second-largest US-based automaker and the fifth-largest in the world based on 2010 vehicle sales. He failed, failed, and failed and paved the way for his success amidst all these failures, but never allowed anything to stop him or his ability to take on challenges!

Failure is simply the opportunity to begin again, this time more intelligently.

~ Henry Ford

Another iconic man who is today regarded as one of America's finest film producers, directors, screenwriters, voice actors, animators, entrepreneurs, entertainers, and philanthropists of all times does not have a very different failure history than Henry Ford and his is far more extensive in numbers:

- Walt Disney was fired by a newspaper editor because 'he lacked imagination and had no good ideas'
- At 22, he experienced bankruptcy after the failure of a cartoon series in Kansas City

- ➜ On the heels of a successful run with Oswald the Lucky Rabbit (one of his successful cartoon characters), Walt learned that not only had his distributors unfairly obtained ownership of the character, but also that most of the artists who worked for him had committed themselves to working for the distributor instead. Essentially, Walt's entire organisation was taken from him, and he was left to fend for himself and start all over again.
- ➜ To replace Oswald, he created a new character in Mickey Mouse and when he tried to get MGM Studios to distribute Mickey Mouse in 1927, he was told that the idea would never work — a giant mouse on the screen would terrify women
- ➜ When he first conceptualized the idea of Disneyland and revealed it to the world, the proposed park was rejected by the city of Anaheim on the grounds that it would only attract riffraff
- ➜ He went bankrupt several times before he built Disneyland, but he persisted

Walt did everything except for giving up! In the long run, surely he has been successful, with more than 81 feature films and hundreds of short films to his credit. He has earned more than 950 honours, including 48 Academy Awards, and 22 Oscar Awards and also founded the California Institute of Arts.

Abraham Lincoln, Henry Ford, or Walt Disney, they all failed several times and then resurrected their lives and their companies/ causes and took it to unimaginable heights. They are well known today for their successes and achievements and not for their temporary setbacks or failures.

Only those who dare to fail greatly can achieve greatly.

~ Robert F. Kennedy

List down all the major failures in your life, a lesson that you learnt from each of them and how different your approach will be when you encounter a similar situation in the future.

Failures	Lesson Learnt	New Approach

'Power of Vengeance': The most crucial characteristic of a leader

The word 'vengeance' often referred to as 'revenge', 'reprisal', or 'settling scores' has a negative connotation in the English language. A vengeful person is often seen in a poor light and considered to be an unforgiving soul determined to take an eye for an eye — a person far from being the leader we have been discussing so far.

And yet it is this same 'vengeance' that is the most crucial ingredient that goes into making a leader. A person without 'inner vengeance' is like a leader who does not have fire in his belly that is required to lead people, solve problems, and change the world. Well, what we are referring to here is the positive impact that vengeance creates in the life of a leader.

Vengeance is private anger that you manufacture within yourself very consciously, very deliberately, to fight back and not accept whatever you are told or accused of.

Let me elaborate this for you.

Vengeance is a private anger that 'you' manufacture. It is not accidental or coincidental or enforced upon you by someone else; it is an extremely conscious and deliberate choice. It's like you were waiting for people to create difficulties for you — for someone to tell you, you cannot do this, this is not your cup of tea — and the moment someone actually tells you what you were waiting to hear, you steer a special kind of anger within you to do exactly what you have been denied or told is not possible at your level.

Though it is a negative attitude that indicates revenge, it channels your inner resolve to prove to the world what you are worthy of. This is known as the 'Power of Vengeance', which is extremely important in a leader. It brings out the toughness, ruthlessness and drive that is required to transform the surroundings and make the world a better place.

Each time I was denied anything because I could not afford it or someone felt I did not deserve it, it only strengthened my inner resolve to achieve it and by using the power of my inner vengeance, I set myself on an even more aggressive drive to do so.

Way back in the 1980s, when I was in my late teens, there lived a guy in my building. We were childhood friends and since we stayed in the same building, we had a cordial relationship. He dropped out of school very early, while I stayed on and completed my graduation. He worked as a spot-selling agent at Candy Wines (a wine shop) and earned a decent commission from that job. In those days, 50cc mopeds had just been introduced and he had recently bought a TVS 50 moped with his earnings. He would park right in front of the building gate. One day, as I was entering the building, I saw him parking his vehicle, my heart suddenly desired to ride it and I requested him for a round on his moped.

He took a moment to scan me from top to bottom making me feel as if I had committed a crime, then looked at his moped, declared loudly the value of that vehicle and said, *'Isko chalane ki teri aukad nahi hai'* which means 'I'm not worthy of it'. That day I decided to work very hard, make a lot of money and purchase my own motorcycle and two months after I joined Eureka Forbes, I proved my worth, broke all records, saved enough money and bought a brand new Rajdoot 175cc telescopic suspension motorbike (far better than my friend's moped) and parked it right next to his vehicle and stood shoulder-to-shoulder with him.

I had been disgraced, humiliated, challenged and pushed to the extremes by my friend, and I used the power of vengeance positively to achieve greater heights in my life.

Once, when I was working in Team Productivity as the Vice President-Operations, my Joint MD, Mr. A. W. George had a meeting with the Vice President at one of the most renowned and respected Indian business houses and asked me to accompany him. This Vice President was a big man, and I grabbed the opportunity. However, when George introduced me as the Vice President of Team Productivity, the man on the other side very curtly said, 'I don't think you can value add to us in any manner. Would you mind waiting outside please, Mr. Nair.'

I decided that day that I would become such a well-known name in the Corporate Training world that this business house would be forced to call me to add value to their staff and following that I executed several workshops for them in the following years.

Similarly, I was shooed away by the Vice President-HR of an Indian luggage conglomerate and the then Sales Controller of a telecommunication giant, whose Secretary walked up to me at the reception where I was waiting for him and told me, 'The Sales Controller does not meet strangers, Mr. Nair. Can you please leave?' And yet one day, all these people were compelled to come back to me to engage my services for their organisations, because I used each of the above instances in my favour to upgrade my own skills and capabilities and create a notorious market reputation of nothing below excellence that they were left with no other options. For several years following each of these incidents, I was the Chief Sales and Leadership trainer for practically all divisions of these companies.

All I can now say is that I am deeply grateful to my friend, that Vice President, the HR Head, that Sales Controller and tens and hundreds of their likes that I have encountered in my life, for had it not been for them and the disgrace and humiliation that they caused me, I would have probably remained an ordinary human being. But because of vengeance and my desire to prove them wrong, I strived to achieve more and that has made me what I am today.

Pen down five incidents in your life where you have been humiliated and write down how you will use the 'Power of Vengeance' to win back your confidence:

Humiliation	Action Plan for Vengeance	Deadline

So does that mean that only if people are put through difficult and challenging situations in life, they emerge as leaders? Then what about Amitabh Bachchan, A.P.J. Abdul Kalam (Former President of India), Steve Jobs, Margaret Thatcher (First lady Prime

Minister of England), Chanda Kochhar (CEO and MD-ICICI Bank, India), Vishwanathan Anand (Chess Grandmaster) and others like them who are considered idols and leaders?

Leaders are people whose life is dedicated to a cause.

Leaders live for a cause — a cause that is bigger than themselves. They have a purpose in life — a purpose that is beyond them, their likes/dislikes, luxuries, lives, and the lives of their close friends and families.

➜ For Thomas Alva Edison, the cause was inventions, inventions, inventions!

➜ For Edmund Hillary, it was climbing Mount Everest

➜ For Sachin Tendulkar, it was excellence in Cricket

➜ For Narayan Murthy, it was building the best IT company in the world

➜ For Henry Ford, it was the invention of the automobile industry.

➜ For Ratan Tata, the cause is Tata & Sons

➜ For Amitabh Bachchan, it is surprising people with his performance

➜ For Zakir Husain, it is creating magic with the tabla

They eat, sleep, drink, breathe, and live their cause. They go beyond their call of duty, explore every aspect of their field, undergo inner struggles, and reach a stage where their names become synonymous with their cause.

Ordinary people deal with problems, they enjoy their lives, get married, have children, travel the world, enjoy luxuries and plan for a sound and stable retirement. While leaders also do all this, it does not become their life, but merely remains a part of their existence, for what drives them is the cause of their living, the purpose of their life.

Your cause should be bigger than you. What is your cause?

Years ago, I came across five questions, which shook me from within and made me realise the ordinariness of my life and for the benefit of you all, I would like to reveal these questions which I now call the Five Magic Questions:

Five Magic Questions

1. Why do you get out of bed every day in the morning?
2. Who are the most important people in your life?
3. What is important for you in your life?
4. What do you really love the most about your life?
5. What would you like to do before you leave this world?

These questions look very simple but they will show you the essence of a leader, and all leaders are Life Maximizers. Many years ago, I asked these questions to myself and the answers have evolved over a period of time.

1. Why do I get out of bed every day in the morning?

Many years ago, I got out of bed every day in the morning to make this world better than it was yesterday.

Today, I get out of bed every day in the morning to build

success stories by enabling people and organisations to rise above their limiting paradigms and thereby thrive in a constantly changing world.

(This incidentally has become the core purpose of my company **smm**art and the cause for the existence of hundreds of people working in **smm**art.)

Read that answer once again. The job that I have set out for will never end! As long as there are human beings on this planet, my work remains in motion — I want to build success stories. How? By enabling people and organisations to rise above their limiting paradigms. What will happen because of that? It will help people thrive, not just survive in a constantly changing world. This endless, timeless work is not just a job, but the purpose of my life and my existence.

This same question, when asked to a non-life maximizer could give varied answers. I have done so in the last 29 years of my professional life and the answers have ranged from one level to the other, for example:

- → I get out of bed every day in the morning to complete my pending work
- → To go to the office/factory
- → Earn a living so that I can feed myself and my family
- → I get out of bed every day in the morning, because I have appointments lined up for the day and people waiting to meet me
- → I get out of bed every day because it is in the morning that I am accustomed to getting out of the bed every day for the last 49 years
- → I get out of bed every day in the morning because I am not sleepy anymore

→ I get out bed every day in the morning because I did not die yesterday

All these people get out of bed to only spend their life. They do not have a cause/purpose to achieve, anything to contribute to the world so that their life becomes meaningful to others.

2. Who are the most important people in your life?

For a non-life maximizer, the answer to this question will be:

→ I, me, myself

→ My wife, my children, my friends, my family

→ My employees, my customers, my suppliers

For me, every human being present on this planet is important and I will do everything possible to transform him/her, to take them closer to his/her goals, to help them lead a more meaningful life, to maximize their lives and thereby transform my own. In short, 'humanity'.

3. What is important for you in your life?

For me, it is important to live a significant and transformational life and contribute to the world. It is important that people take on challenges because I came into their lives, that I live a life of vitality, energy and passion and help people live a life of abundance, achievement, and glory. It is important that people believe in themselves and their capabilities and maximize themselves to the fullest; I give back more than what I receive from anywhere; I don't quit when faced with challenges and obstacles; I empower people and help them achieve their dreams, vision, and goals in life. It is important for me to make people think and enlighten them about themselves, their present and their future through extremely powerful and inspiring communication. Ultimately, I want to instill in them the freedom, liberation and confidence to act.

For a non-life maximizer, the answer to this question could be:

It is important for me to come back home by 6 pm; live a life of peace and happiness with my family and friends; retire by 50; spend the rest of my life in a small farmhouse away from the city; travel the world; enjoy the best luxuries, comfort, and wealth, etc.

I don't know what your answer to this question is. If you are a life maximizer (you ought to be), you will have a bigger and better answer than that — one that goes beyond your wants, desires, and comforts. If you don't, then change the reason for your existence from this moment.

4. What do you really love the most about your life?

➜ What I love the most about my life is that in the last 29 years I have never told a single lie to my customers while selling.

➜ I always was on time for every client appointment throughout my life.

➜ I have remained productive under the most frustrating and challenging conditions in life.

➜ Each year I made more money, name, fame, respect, and reputation than the previous year.

➜ I gave a beautiful life to my parents, wife, children and all those who were close to me.

➜ I never remained static and continuously challenged the status quo around me on a daily, weekly, hourly basis.

- I consistently upgraded my knowledge, transformed my attitudes, developed a whole lot of skills, formed new and progressive habits and changed all strategies to live life and run business year after year.
- I surrendered myself unconditionally to all my goals.
- I never gave reasons for non-performance.
- I respected all my bosses throughout my professional life.
- I was India's No. 1 vacuum cleaner salesman for Eureka Forbes, No. 1 Group Leader, No. 1 Sales Supervisor, No. 1 Branch Manager and the No. 1 in everything that I did in my personal and professional life.
- I have been tough with myself and others all my life.
- I made thousands of people believe in themselves, demanded the best from people, loved them, cared for them, gave away my knowledge unconditionally and allowed them to win.
- I was never afraid that someone would learn from me, go away and make it bigger than me in life.
- I am unafraid of failure and can speak about it with courage and conviction.
- What I love about my life is that I have trained over two million people and left a lasting impression and mark on their lives for a lifetime.
- I have created millions of possibility thinkers, changed the thoughts, words and deeds of people around me.
- I have been loved, respected, and taken care of by millions of people.
- I am not tired even after working hard for 29 long years.

- At 49, I am still young, charged up, excited and raring to go, taking on more and more with each new day of my life.
- I am still a fighter.
- I have a role model mother, a loving wife, fantastic children, great colleagues and subordinates, ever-supportive customers, vendors, suppliers and innumerable well-wishers... and the list can just go on and on.

What is it that you love the most about your life? I am sure you have a list which can go on and on for a few pages, if not more and you must ask this question daily, weekly, monthly, quarterly, yearly, decade after decade... and if you don't love many things about your life, your visit to this planet has been a waste. Your life has been insignificant and:

An insignificant life inspires none.

5. What would you like to do before you leave this world?

If you ask me, I can open an entire Pandora's Box. Before I leave this world, I want to:

- Write a hundred books
- Create a thousand audios, videos
- Become a talk show host
- Learn ten new languages
- Act in five movies
- Build a studio of my own

- Make my audios and videos available worldwide through Santosh Nair's knowledge products and merchandise company
- Make **smm**art the world's finest individual/entrepreneur/ enterprise transformation company
- Build the **smm**art Township for all our employees to stay together and grow old together
- Form the **smm**art Foundation to cater to the needs of underprivileged children and women and instill in them the spirit of entrepreneurship
- Create a bright and glorious future for all the employees, partners and associates of **smm**art
- Give their children the best education
- Create the Santosh Nair's Sales, Leadership and T.I.G.E.R. Club for the mental and physical rejuvenation of people across the world
- Travel around the world educating people to become fearless and confident
- Help people transcend their accidental origins
- Make people future-focused and self-transformative, help them thrive on change
- Work with the United Nations, speak to the prime ministers and presidents of the world
- Be the chief negotiator amongst warring factions
- Bring peace between countries — Pakistan, the Middle East, etc.
- Form long-lasting, sustainable peace at the world level
- Make India and Pakistan one nation
- Teach people the ill-effects of technology

- ➜ Speak at national and international fora all over the world
- ➜ Eradicate poverty from India and the world
- ➜ Become the original thinker of solutions to at least thousand issues that are troubling the world
- ➜ Remain active and young till I die at the age of 120
- ➜ Ultimately become a role model for the world to believe in, look up to, and emulate.

Have you asked yourself these five magic questions? If you have not, then today is a beautiful day to begin this new life. Ask yourself these questions and get answers that make life worth living. Implement these answers in your life and make them come true. Make life meaningful and significant and contribute to the world. You will love yourself and the world for that. Go for it!

Why do you get out of bed every day in the morning?

____

____

____

____

____

____

____

____

____

____

____

____

Who are the most important people in your life?

What is important for you in your life?

What do you really love the most about your life?

What would you like to do before you leave this world?

While living an extraordinary life, there are a few leaders who surpass the idea of leadership and go far beyond it to emerge as role models.

Role models are the highest version of leaders. They are disturbed, upset, and enraged by injustice, and wrongdoings around them and take it upon themselves to transform the world. People like Anna Hazare who was disturbed by the rising corruption in India, has taken it upon himself to create a corruption-free nation. Mahatma Jyotiba Phule was upset about the inequalities that prevailed between boys and girls fought for women education and empowerment way back in 1848. Dr. Babasaheb Ambedkar was enraged by the Hindu caste system and the social discrimination practices that categorised few of the lower class Hindu sects as untouchables and strived for the dalits to be treated with fairness, equal respect, and honour, thus eradicating the concept of 'untouchables' forever.

Role models do not have a family, home, or life of their own. Their nation is their home, their countrymen their family, and their cause is their life. They leave behind all their worldly riches, luxuries, desires, business, career, and profession for the quest of fulfilling their cause and do not even fear death. They always have a choice between living as the father of four children or becoming the father of the nation; and they invariably choose the latter like Mahatma Gandhi.

When you are a role model, people surrender themselves to you and your cause.

Way back on 7 June, 1893, an England-educated law practitioner in South Africa was travelling with a first class ticket in an upcountry train from Durban (South Africa) to Pretoria (the capital of the Dutch-governed Transvaal province of South Africa). A European railway official asked him to shift to the third class compartment because he was Indian, since 'coolies' and non-whites were apparently not permitted in first class compartments. When he refused, the young man was thrown out of the train and his luggage tossed out on the platform. That day, a man was disturbed, upset, and enraged by the injustice around him. He took it upon himself to transform the world and emerged Mahatma Gandhi who gave up his law practice and served a 21-year long tenure fighting against racial discrimination for the rights of the Indian community in South Africa and then came back to his homeland to win freedom for India.

In the 1940s, a schoolteacher was walking down the streets of Kolkata (India) when she saw a destitute woman crying for help. Knowing that this woman was about to die, she rushed to the hospital where she was told to sit and wait. Her critical situation was so dire that she was immediately rushed to another hospital, but again the woman's lower class status put her at the bottom of the patient list. Later that night, the woman died in the arms of this schoolteacher. That day, an ordinary nun was disturbed, upset and enraged by her helplessness and there emerged Mother Teresa who dedicated her life to the welfare and upliftment of the sick and the poor and helping the terminally ill embrace a death of dignity, if not life.

Far away from this Catholic schoolteacher was another lawyer, the son of a wealthy landlord in the Wardha district of Maharashtra (India). Brought up with all the luxuries and wealth in the world, he possessed his own gun since 14 and was given a Singer sports car with cushions covered with panther skin when he was old enough to drive. With a keen interest in cinema, he would purchase two tickets whenever he went to watch a film — one in the front and one in the back — the back one to sit on and the front one so he could stretch his legs — such was his extravagance. And one fine day, at the corner of a street, getting drenched in the heavy rain, he saw a man suffering from leprosy take his last breath. That sight sent shivers up and down his spine. His worldly luxuries and wealth suddenly became irrelevant, he was shaken up from within and emerged as Baba Amte who gave up his family profession and devoted his entire life to the rehabilitation and empowerment of people suffering from leprosy.

All these people have common traits and qualities. Each of these people:

1. Rose above their opposition, crisis, and personal tragedies
2. They directed ordinary people through challenging times
3. They took on other people's challenges and made them win
4. They took charge of the situation when others were confused and clueless
5. They were accountable for their deeds
6. They all did Halla Bol — stood for what they felt was right

These are the characteristics or attributes of a role model that need to be imbibed. There is a very thin line between leaders and role models. It is a journey, a gradual progression from being a leader to being a role model where your bungalow, your S-Class Mercedes, private jet, multi-million dollar business, Rolex watch, three-piece tuxedo, all seems insignificant. All these men and women have been leaders in their lives before they decided to dedicate their life to their cause 100% and this is how they moved from being leaders to becoming role models.

I consider myself somewhere in between a leader and a role model striving to reach the stature of a role model where I will renounce all my worldly riches, luxuries, and desires and travel to the interiors of India — the remote, education deprived places where I will awaken the young men and women to realise their true potential and reach their dreams. India as a nation will become a developed country owing to the endless work that I would have done for the youth of tomorrow that live in rural India. It is a long journey but I shall make it happen, for I am a Life Maximizer.

The life described above is the life of a leader — on the way to becoming a role model — and a life worth living. Being a leader and declaring that you will be a leader for life is essential and compulsory for Life Maximization.

In order to maximize life for a lifetime, you need to give this order, this instruction, this directive, this mandate, this law of God, this commandment every day, every hour, every minute of your life. The seventh of the Eleven Commandments is:

Declare that you will be a leader for life.

8

Say Goodbye to E.D.D.

(Emotionally Draining Distractions)

Excessive emotions interfere with intelligence.

Part – I

Sachin Tendulkar, the leading Indian batsman was playing in the 1999 Cricket World Cup, when he received the news of his father's untimely demise. In a state of shock, Tendulkar flew back to India to perform the final rites for his father. Three days later was India's match against Kenya, an important match that required the leading batsman of the nation on the pitch. Tendulkar packed his bags and was on his way to play for his country within 72 hours of living through the biggest loss of his life. He returned with a bang to the World Cup scoring a century — an unbeaten 140 off 101 balls — his best innings ever. He dedicated this century to his father. He made his team proud, his nation proud, and most of all, his father proud.

Virat Kohli, the new Indian batting sensation lost his father on 19 December, 2006 at two in the morning, in the middle of a crucial Ranji trophy tie against Karnataka where Virat was the overnight batsman for Delhi. His team — a bunch of sensitive, caring and nice human beings — urged him to return to his family, but he knew his presence was essential for their victory. Torn between his commitment towards his game and state and his family, the 18-year old Virat Kohli decided to stay back and bat for his state. Not only did he play that night, but he hit an unbelievable 90, driving his team to victory and came directly to the funeral after his knock of 90. This match marked the turning point in his life!

Anu Agha, the former Chairperson of Thermax (a Pune-based engineering firm) was asked to take on the mantle of Chairmanship after her husband's sudden death in 1996. The board decided that the family business started by her father and built by her husband over the years into a nationally reputed engineering company, now needed her direction and she was there to take over the reins within 48 hours of her husband's demise. She did not even have the time to mourn. Within a year she lost her only son in a car accident as he was returning after a business meeting. She still held fort and continued her professional responsibilities with equal amount of dedication and vigour. Within a week she lost her mother-in-law and her beloved pet dog — enough traumas for a 55-year-old woman.

She did take a call on her life in the most gracious and dignified manner by re-dedicating herself to the cause of turning around Thermax. She brought in foreign consultants, restructured the company, reconstituted the board and improved performance several-fold making Thermax a leading manufacturer of engineering products and systems for industries with its presence in over 14 countries, which earned her several business awards and a position in the list of 25 most powerful women in business.

Were Tendulkar and Kohli unaffected by the deaths of their fathers, or did Anu Agha not love her family enough? Well, an ordinary human being may think this way, but only a Life Maximizer can understand the magnanimity and grace they exhibited.

The world around us is full of problems. There isn't a single man who is free of worries, troubles and grief. Rich or poor, contemporary or conventional, aged or young, people are often faced with weak moments in life — moments that sadden them, break them, shake them from within and shatter them completely. This could be the loss of a loved one, a family tragedy, a dispute in the family, an ageing parent diagnosed with a terminal illness, a marital discord leading to separation, a betrayal by a friend, your guy walking out on you, your husband cheating on you with your best friend, the murder of your child... the list can just keep going on and on.

All these horrible events have occurred to me or someone close to me. These are all events that can hold you back from performing to the best of your abilities. They can blind you to the world and what it has in store for you. It can derail you from reaching your true worth in life, make you stagnate, distract you from your purpose in life, and keep you like a mere Wandering Generality, disallowing you from becoming a Meaningful Specific ever. It can entangle you in the complexities of the present deterring you from envisioning a better future and chasing your cause for existence.

In my world of Life Maximization, I call these events:

EDD i.e. Emotionally Draining Distractions

As the name suggests, Emotionally Draining Distractions refer to those events that emotionally drain you, handicapping your mind and leaving you vulnerable forever. The more you remain in this state, the farther you get from life maximization.

A death in an Indian family entails observing certain rituals for a minimum of 13 days forbidding the family from indulging in any kind of worldly affairs. If a divorce is a major event it can plunge a person into depression for weeks and months. An illness if taken too seriously can become bigger than death itself.

Closing yourself to the world during such times, shutting shop, and remaining in that moment for a long time can make life itself a difficult journey, let alone maximization.

If Sachin Tendulkar kept wondering why his father had died, he would have lost his edge as a cricketer; if Virat Kohli sat next to his father's ashes for days together, it would have killed his spirit; if Anu Agha cursed her destiny for such a tragic life, she would have never been able to realise her own true potential.

For each of these people, life fell apart when they encountered these situations and why would it not; after all they were emotionally challenging moments. But as I've said, **'excessive**

emotions interfere with intelligence'. These people held on to their emotions, but were steady about their purpose. They did not allow these emotional moments to overpower their intelligence and maximized life for themselves!

The beauty of today's tragedy is that it reduces the pain of yesterday's tragedy.

As long as one keeps these EDDs intact in one's life, Life Maximization can never happen. For Life Maximization, you have to say goodbye to EDD.

While I am not saying that one must not bother about such serious events or treat them as trifling problems, they should not overpower the purpose of your living. Life cannot stop and hence, they say, 'The show must go on….'

In his CD called *Winning Zig Ziglar* one of the greatest inspirational speakers of the world explains a concept called '24 hours'. Any event in your life — big or small, tragic or joyous, victorious or defeating, failure or achievement, criticism or acclaim — should not be entertained for more than 24 hours. Whatever the extent or the intensity of the matter, do not give more than 24 hours to anything in life! Be in that moment for 24 hours, but as the 25th hour begins, get up, and start afresh.

Brushing aside your professional life for something that has collapsed in your personal life, is like breaking the walls in your ship that will bring you to the shore once the waves die down. When one aspect of life defeats you, focus even more strongly on the other. Engross yourself in work, hobbies, people, society etc. Strive to achieve your purpose like never before, chase your dreams with more conviction than you ever have and rededicate yourself to your purpose. Do things that give you pleasure, find solace in your job, get so involved in life that there is no time left to even dwell on your grief, let alone express it.

You can't bring back what is gone or undo what has already happened, but what you can do is build a better tomorrow. You have no control over your past, but the future is still in your hands. So what are you waiting for? Transcend the grief brought about by your personal tragedies and build your situation back, build your circumstances back, build your life back!

I lost my father when I was in Dubai, attending the wedding of a friend's daughter. When I was informed about it by my family in India, I rushed home with my wife Sindhu, took charge of the situation, performed the last rites and gave a ceremonious farewell to the man who taught me some of the finest lessons of my life. Two days later, I had to address a group of people for Tata Housing in Goa; not that Tata Housing would have blacklisted me for my absence on grounds of personal reasons, but I had taken money for this programme, had committed my presence and hundreds of people from all over the country were coming there to listen to me.

Against the advice of many, I took the first flight out and was in front of the audience motivating them for higher performance. Barely a year later, I lost my elder brother-in-law and my actions were no different. My wife met with a major accident, all my three daughters — Devika, Malavika, Radhika were born while I was addressing a training programme, but none of these instances — tragedies or moments of joy — distracted me from pursuing my cause as a trainer or a motivational speaker.

Did I love my father any less, was the death of my brother-in-law unimportant, or did I not value my wife and the birth of my three children? Certainly not! But I am a Life Maximizer, I had instructed myself, commanded, ordered, demanded that I would stay away from EDDs and not allow any personal or professional tragedy or joyous moment to derail my life.

In the middle of the big things that you are trying to do, the birth of your children will take place, several tragedies could occur. If you are available on that day, you must be with your child, but if you have a commitment to be honoured, that shouldn't be set aside because a public commitment made is far bigger than a private tragedy/joy and that ought to be given more value if you have to be a Life Maximizer.

Write down three EDDs that you are currently undergoing and construct an action plan to come out of it.

No.	EDD	Action Plan
1		
2		
3		

In order to maximize life for a lifetime, you need to give this order, this instruction, this directive, this mandate, this law of God, this commandment every day, every hour, every minute of your life:

Say goodbye to emotionally draining distractions.

Part – II

We have to produce maximum results in minimum time and maximum results with minimum efforts. At work or at home we can be productive only if we do not get carried away by distractions. Irritation, anxiety, anger, frustration, hurt, unhappiness, jealousy, suspicion, hostility, guilt, helplessness, depression, rejection, neglect, ego, greed etc. are all 100% distractions. Once we start feeling any or all of these emotions, our focus shifts from our goals. To remain productive despite the most frustrating conditions of life, one has to be conscious of our emotions.

Some emotions help you fight, and move forward… these are energy boosting emotions.

On the other hand, some emotions make you gloomy, angry, frustrated, anxious, guilty… these are energy draining, self-destructive emotions.

Emotions decide the state of your mind and the state of your well being when things go wrong in life. And things do go wrong, so what should your emotions be at such times?

I have always said that you should be possessed by the following four emotions or states of mind.

- ➜ Sense of Humour
- ➜ Cheerfulness
- ➜ Self-confidence
- ➜ Enthusiasm

These are the hallmarks of a Life Maximizer.

You need to declare that whatever happens in life:

1. **I will not allow my sense of humour to dwindle. I will always keep it alive!**

   To solve problems, you need to have a sense of humour — the ability to laugh at yourself and the whole world. You need to be amused with life and everything that life offers, good or bad.

2. **I will remain cheerful — happy and ready to create or manufacture the next big thing after a debacle!**

   To solve problems, you need to be cheerful — the ability to remain in good spirits at all times, be optimistic, bright, and pleasant.

3. **I will be confident and remind myself that it is confidence and confidence alone that will help me learn anything, adjust to anything, and accomplish anything in life!**

   Without confidence, especially when things are not in your favour, you will not be in a position to direct your thoughts, words, and deeds to achieve the next big goal after a downfall.

4. **I will remain enthusiastic, vibrant, and excited about life. I will constantly remind myself that even though many things around me are shattered, I still have a lot of things intact in life with bigger goals to achieve!**

   To solve problems you need to be enthusiastic. I was told many years ago, that an enthusiast is a man possessed by God. Therefore, you should come across as though you are possessed by God.

Your personality should be such that when people see you, interact with you, they should feel that you are shouting out for joy. On looking at you, people should forget their miseries. Your existence should give comfort and peace to everyone. Meeting you should be like a festival — a celebration, a moment to rejoice.

What is your method in the madness of life?

The method is your declaration that, *'I will be ruled by the right emotions in life; even in the most frustrating circumstances.'* As William Shakespeare said, 'Nothing in the world is good or bad… thinking makes it so.'

We are all intelligent people; whether we are wise or not is debatable though. So let us proceed with the notion that we are all intelligent people.

This means that we have the ability to eliminate our problems, get out of difficult situations, and resurrect our lives when faced with tragedies and obstacles. However, in a career spanning 29 glorious years, I have seen the most intelligent people doing the most stupid things and breaking down. Ever wondered why this happens?

Well, they are all filled with emotions that don't allow them to move forward. Emotions like anxiety, guilt, hostility, depression, frustration, anger, dejection, and so on. These emotions are manufactured because of the demands that we make from our ecosystem.

Our ecosystem consists of people and things. Now if you know 'people' and if you know 'things', they often go wrong. Our ecosystem unfortunately also consists of us. So if I have to sum it up, our ecosystem consists of us, others, and the things around us.

The biggest problem is the demands we have from all these three constituents:

The first ecosystem demand is that 'I must be perfect'.

The second ecosystem demand is that 'others around me must be perfect'.

The third ecosystem demand is that 'the things around me must be perfect'.

Now there is a problem here:

Demands vs. Expectations

Demands are the claims that you make on the ecosystem — it is something you want and assert your right to have it. Expectations on the other hand are your desires, and you would be happy if fulfilled.

So we can either demand something from ourselves, others, and the things around us, or we can expect something from ourselves, others, and the things around us. The problem is the demand. If we had expectations instead of demands we would have continued to function with our four useful emotions — cheerfulness, self-confidence, enthusiasm, and a sense of humour.

All Life Maximizers, because of their own experiences and that of others, have realised that human beings are imperfect people living in an equally imperfect world. Demanding perfection from people living in an imperfect world is not only foolish but also a guaranteed formula for derailment from one's purpose. Life Maximizers have also realised that 'things' will and can go wrong and therefore to 'demand' that things must happen as per one's demands is too farfetched!

Ecosystem Demand No. 1

You demand perfection from yourself and this leads to irrational self-beliefs:

- ➜ I must make everybody happy
- ➜ I must be prepared for anything
- ➜ My children must respect me
- ➜ My colleagues must respect me
- ➜ I must complete all 20 activities assigned to me today (when actually you cannot even do five)
- ➜ I must not say no to anything
- ➜ I must be useful and worthy to others
- ➜ I must not make any mistakes
- ➜ I must have control over myself
- ➜ I must be a perfect son, a perfect daughter, a prefect wife, a perfect husband, a perfect brother, a perfect father, a perfect boss, a perfect subordinate, a perfect daughter-in-law, a perfect mother, a perfect human being.

People who are dominated by these thoughts of perfection suffer from anxiety and guilt:

1. **Anxiety about their future**
2. **Guilt about their past**

For example, a student demands perfection from himself and says 'I must get 96% and win the appreciation of my teachers, principal, parents, friends, etc.' If he ends up getting 85%, he is unable to accept this and anxiety sets in. He starts negative self-talk, 'What will happen to my future? My life is useless, my life is ruined. What will people think about me? How can I face the world? How can I face my parents? This life is not worth living.'

This could lead to self-destructive actions like suicide, which has become quite common in recent times.

These people are anxious about their future and this anxiety interferes with their intelligence and they end up ruining their careers and lives. Once again, let me remind you:

Excessive emotions interfere with intelligence.

The 'I must be perfect' people are always living in the future and their emotions are dictated by events around them. If those events are not according to their so-called 'perfect standards' they get angry with themselves and once anger (a negative emotion) sets in, they cannot focus, function, or concentrate on life. This handicaps them, and all actions and decisions that follow are an outcome of their emotions.

Professionals who demand perfection in life suffer from similar emotions:

➔ I must make a perfect presentation

➔ I must not make any mistakes at work

➔ I must be the best at whatever I do

➔ I must be appreciated for my commitment, passion, and dedication. If I don't get this appreciation I am useless.

Any human being dictated by anxiety and perfectionism cannot balance himself when things don't match up to his standards of perfection. Let me tell you my dear friends, you are not going to be perfect always.

These people who demand perfection from themselves cannot say no to anyone or anything. You go to them with any kind of a job/task and ask them to do it, they will readily take it up because they are obsessed with the idea of being perfect. They cannot refuse. And because they cannot say 'no', they take on more on their platter than what they can actually chew and when you take on more than you can handle, you are bound to make errors.

When such perfectionists make errors, they suffer from one more emotion — guilt. Guilt about the past — why did I take up this job, why didn't I say no, etc.

Thus, people who demand perfection from themselves suffer from two emotions:

1. **Guilt about the Past**
2. **Anxiety about the Future**

Because of this they remain emotionally drained and distracted and a person who is emotionally drained and distracted can never be a Life Maximizer.

Ecosystem Demand No. 2

You demand perfection from others and when you demand perfection from others, these thoughts run in your mind:

➜ Others must be just and kind to me

➜ Others must help me

➜ They must understand me

- They must know my challenges and difficulties and give me only what I can handle
- Others must love me unconditionally
- They must not be demanding
- They must value my judgment, my views, my ideas and thoughts
- People on the roads must not cut lanes and overtake me while I am driving
- My wife must inform me before going out
- She must support me in my business venture
- She must understand me and respect my views every time… all the time
- My daughter must be an extrovert
- My son must realise that I will be disheartened if he does not get 95%. Therefore, he must get 95%
- He must not be on Facebook all the time
- My children must be well-behaved in front of my friends and guests
- My boss must understand my challenges at home and not load me with new jobs
- My subordinates must work hard and not go home till they finish the assignment given to them
- They must not make mistakes
- They must be dedicated, loyal, and committed all the time

- → My colleagues must tell me everything
- → I must not be questioned by my boss or colleagues
- → My partners must not be selfish and self centered
- → They must not do anything that I don't like
- → My company must not transfer me
- → My company must help me in times of difficulty
- → My commission must be paid on time irrespective of the difficulties that my organisation is facing
- → My target must not be increased in the middle of the year
- → I must get my promotion even when I have not done everything that was expected from me
- → Nobody must be against me, else I am worthless.

Because of this demand of perfection from others, people suffer from two emotions:

1. Hostility
2. Depression

Hostility

When those around you do not operate as per your perfectionist standards, you become hostile and angry with others since they just don't seem to understand you and your feelings. You can get really violent and aggressive in such situations. You can end up killing people, hitting them, hurting them, destroying things. Most murders even by the most rational and sane people happen during such moments of anger. Road rage, where people get off their cars to fight, quarrels with vegetable vendors over a few paise, arguments with bartenders or waiters in restaurants, etc. are all outcomes of such hostility and anger.

Depression

Over a period of time when a series of negative incidents happen in these people's lives, and they feel that others, i.e. their sons, daughters, spouse, subordinates, friends, communities, family members etc. do not seem to be aligning with their thoughts or views, they get into another dangerous emotion called depression.

They experience a sense of worthlessness. They become sad, demoralised and such emotions drain their energy and they lose their four positive emotions or state of mind:

1. They lose their sense of humour which is so important to move ahead
2. They are unable to remain cheerful
3. They doubt their own capabilities and lose their self-confidence
4. They are unable to keep their enthusiasm alive and are dictated by the difficulties and circumstances that people create for them

A person dictated by hostility and depression can never be a Life Maximizer!

He loses the ability of accepting, adjusting, and appreciating people — the three most important qualities of a Life Maximizer that we have looked at in Commandment 5.

Ecosystem Demand No. 3

You expect perfection from things around you, not people. And when your mind is dominated by this demand, such will be your thoughts:

- ➜ When I go on the road there must not be any traffic
- ➜ There must not be any potholes
- ➜ There mustn't be competition in my business
- ➜ The government must take measures to make life easy for its citizens
- ➜ My company must give Saturday and Sunday off
- ➜ If possible, they must also give Friday off
- ➜ Since I get up at 10 am, my company must allow me to start work at 12, instead of 9.30
- ➜ The lift must work when I enter it
- ➜ I must get parking space when I go shopping
- ➜ The weather must be 16 degrees, since I don't like anything above or below 16 degrees
- ➜ It must not rain when I am travelling
- ➜ The train must arrive on time
- ➜ The world must understand me and create situations or circumstances that are conducive to me

These people will feel extreme negative emotions including irritation, annoyance, etc. The extent to which they can put up with these emotions makes all the difference. For some people, the ability to accept these emotions is high and for some it is low.

People who have low acceptance of things that could go wrong, cannot bear anything that is not according to their wishes. They cannot handle the '3As', i.e. they cannot accept things as they are; adjust to situations, and appreciate all the beautiful things in this world. They are irritated, upset, disturbed, and angry most of the time through most situations. **They are constantly emotionally drained and distracted.**

On the other hand, people who have a high acceptance of things that could go wrong, can bear extreme irritation, annoyance, and yet remain calm, composed, alert and steady in their thoughts, words, and deeds. They have accepted the fact that they cannot be perfect. They have adjusted to the imperfections of the world and have mastered the art of appreciating all that this world has to offer. **They are Life Maximizers.**

All of us weigh each of these three ecosystem demands differently. At different times in life, depending on our ability to handle our emotions, one of them is dominant.

People suffering from Ecosystem Demand No. 1 will demand certainty about themselves in an uncertain world and as a result:

- ► They regret everything about themselves
- ► They act submissive
- ► They are highly unjust to themselves
- ► They suffer every time
- ► They get upset and depressed that the world has exploited them

People suffering from Ecosystem Demand No. 2 are unable to

get along with people because of their demand of perfection from others, as a result:

- ► They don't care about others
- ► They are impatient with people

People suffering from Ecosystem Demand No. 3 do not want to face any discomfort in life, as a result:

- ► They postpone everything for a perfect time tomorrow
- ► They are constantly discouraged and frustrated by the world

If you don't want to drain yourself emotionally and want to stay focused along the path of success and life maximization, my advice to people is:

Dealing with Ecosystem Demand No. 1

1. Be assertive. Say no when you have to.
2. Displease people by saying 'no' if you are unable to do things as per their demands; that way people know that you possess the ability to say 'no.' Remember these golden words:
   - ► You cannot please all the people, all the time.
   - ► You cannot even please one person, all the time.
3. Ask what you want to ask and get what you want. Don't be afraid of asking merely because you don't want to be rejected.
4. Make yourself happy first
5. Love yourself. That way you will have at least one person loving you.

Dealing with Ecosystem Demand No. 2

1. Understand that people have their own identity, pace, and style of working. Allow people to work according to that.
2. Be patient with others
3. Set expectations in consultation with others to avoid disappointments later
4. Anticipate disobedience/non-compliance and be ready for it
5. Do not do things to others that you won't like to be done to yourself

Dealing with Ecosystem Demand No. 3

1. Understand that successful people and Life Maximizers have great ability to accept things that go wrong and move on
2. Remember conditions in the world were never better than this. You have the best things in the world today in all aspects and areas of life. Enjoy it!
3. The time to do anything is now. Don't delay it. Go for it!
4. Physical, mental, emotional, and psychological pain is the key to any significant achievement

Which of these three ecosystem demands is dominant in your personality? Explain with four examples.

In the table on the opposite page, rewrite the four perfections that you demand from yourself / others/things and the steps will you take to get rid of these demands

No.	Perfections that you demand	Steps you will take to get rid of them	How will you do it?
1			
2			
3			
4			

Problems with Ecosystem Demands

My dear friends, our intelligence, experience and wisdom are tools for problem solving.

Excessive emotions, as I said in the beginning, create interference in our problem solving ability. If we did not make demands on our ecosystem, we could have solved many, many challenges and problems without being derailed. We would have developed the ability to say 'no'; we would have developed the ability to say goodbye to emotionally draining distractions.

The moment we start 'demanding' instead of 'expecting', it gives birth to irrational and negative self-talk and the moment that happens, we are derailed from reaching our destination. So whether it is you, other people, or things, you need to be focused, your aspirations and ambitions are what matter and in order to do that, you need to give this order, this instruction, this directive, this mandate, this law of God, this commandment every day, every hour, every minute of your life:

Say goodbye to emotionally draining distractions.

COMMANDMENT 9

Be ready to be a loner

You have to be abnormal to be a Life Maximizer.

I sometimes feel I am an abnormal species on this earth. My thoughts, philosophies, ideologies are way too different from those people in my immediate ecosystem. I want to upgrade every office assistant in my company. I have a dream that my office helper Mumtaz should set up her own tea stall and provide tea to all the offices in my vicinity. I am on a mission to transform all my MSME (micro, small and medium scale enterprises) clients into world-class corporations — to make a Spartan (a INR 95 crore construction equipment trading and manufacturing company) a Caterpillar Inc. (the world's largest manufacturer of construction and mining equipment with a revenue of over USD 60 bn), a Walplast (a INR 300 crore wall putty company) into an Asian Paints (one of the largest paint companies in India), a Goldmine (a INR 20 crore interior designing and architectural firm) into a Zaha Hadid Architecture (a renowned London-based architectural and interior designing firm known for their contemporary, modern, and out-of-the world creations). I believe all operations of **smm**art can be outsourced and **smm**art can run on a very low cost-high profitability model. I want every employee of **smm**art to become a partner in the company and co-own it with me. I want to provide in-house entrepreneurial opportunities to all interested candidates in my team and keep them hooked with me for a lifetime. I dream of growing old with my employees and staying together in what we call the **smm**art Township. I believe the vegetable hawker sitting just outside the lane I live in, can become an entrepreneur in her own right, set up a chain of vegetable hawkers and run a successful business that assures continuance and perpetuity and there is a strong urge to help her make that happen. I want to reunite the once united nations India and Pakistan and make it one country... the list goes on and on.

Very rarely have I got a taker for these thoughts. People within my company and even those in leadership positions sometimes find it difficult to identify with these thoughts and I ask myself — is something wrong with them or does the problem lie with me?

The only answer to this question can be framed like this:

Life Maximizers are loners in their journey towards Life Maximization.

A Life Maximizer is like an engine driving the train towards a particular destination. People board the train at different stations, make commitments to stay for long, sometimes stay till they reach their destination, and sometimes get down midway. Some may be there for a short distance, some may alight at the very next stop and some may continue till eternity. Regardless of the people who board or alight in due course, the engine continues its journey at its pace as it is the engine that drives the train and not the people on it.

A lot of people have been with me along my journey — some said they would stay for life and got down at the very next station; some said they would get down at the next station and stayed back for a longer while, and some are with me since the start. I never took offense at people who said they would get down at the next station, not allowing them to come along and neither did I take it too seriously when people said they would stay with me for long, believing that they would be with me for life. Either ways, I would have only hindered the process of life maximization for myself — if I started believing that people would be with me for life, I would be shattered when they left (which is inevitable); and on the other hand if I did not allow people to come along because they were already thinking about getting off even as they got on, I would not have been able to bring out their best which would have affected the maximization of my life as well. So, I allowed people to join me at their convenience, unconcerned with the longevity of their association and did the best that I could in the time that I had with them to maximize them and myself.

And the Life Maximizer that I am, I continue to be the engine and pull the bogies with me even today, unaffected by who is coming and who has already left. The engine, though attached to all the bogies, in some manner still remains detached. The power of the engine is more than the power of all the bogies put together. In the absence of an engine, the bogies stand still, but without one or even all bogies, the engine can still reach its destination.

While the world out there is standing to laugh, be a critic, make comments, no one is ready to come forward and drive the train. That charge is solely taken by the engine. Thus, the engine brings meaning to life, clarity to confusion, power to the powerless, direction to the directionless, inspiration to the demotivated, confidence to the weak, capability to the incapable, and so on. It is a life of direction, accountability, and leadership. It is a responsibility, not a privilege, and the engine is always alone in this journey. And therefore, many years ago, I declared to myself that I would never be that bogie, but would be an engine throughout my life. And to be an engine you have to be ready to be a loner in life!

Whilst on this mission, one may go through tremendous self-doubt, hesitation, uncertainty and disbelief, fighting a battle against the world. As I've said earlier, 95% of the world's population is a Wandering Generality and a mere 5% — Meaningful Specific. With that argument when you look around, the world is full of ordinary people, living ordinary lives with ordinary means. They have challenged nothing in their lives and continue living in the status quo for decades. They are the crowd. They are the mob and what is the beauty of the crowd or mob?

A crowd is a group of wounded people; it is hidden in numbers. It cannot give direction, hope or confidence to others; it needs the support of the masters. It doesn't have any principles, philosophies or views of its own. It doesn't have a thought or strategies of its own. It doesn't have a face, it is masked. It has remained the same for decades and will remain the same for centuries to come.

The crowd believes in doing the bare minimum, not taking risks and playing a safe game. They prefer doing what is the accepted norm, following set patterns and doing what everybody else does as they lack the confidence and the courage to stand out and do something different. They like the safety that this facelessness provides and are unwilling to say, do or even think anything that can spin them away from this shield.

Life Maximizers know that as long as they remain a part of the mob, the person in them will never awaken. They will continue leading an ordinary life with thoughts, words, and philosophies that are influenced by others. Their originality will never come to the fore and they will get lost as part of the crowd. They will bring about no change in this world, they will make no difference, their coming to this planet and leaving will have no significance and they will never be able to maximize life.

And so, in order to maximize life, they take a very mindful, conscious decision to stand out from the crowd. They know that their thoughts, philosophies, and decisions will not match that of the world but what they also know is that the world needs their radical thinking, the world needs their bizarre philosophies and their bold decisions, for it is only this radical thinking, bizarre philosophies, and bold decisions that pave the way for a better life, start the next revolution and make this world a better place.

In 1998, Ratan Tata, the chairman of the Tata Group was running Tata Motors and decided to buy JLR (Jaguar & Land

Rover), a loss-making unit for the last 19 years, which could have dissolved Tata Motors and toss the Tata brand on its head. It was an act no sane man would have undertaken. He would have surely faced opposition from his own people, but the maverick Ratan Tata with his vision and spirit of a loner pushed through and bought JLR. Today it has saved Tata Motors by contributing to two-thirds of their revenue and three-fourth of their profits.

Soon after this experience, in 2009, when all the automobile giants were focusing on bigger luxury cars, Ratan Tata launched Tata Nano — the world's most affordable car for the middle class, which put at stake the entire credibility of Tata Motors. With the obvious technical limitations on one side (due to the low cost) and the political pressures on the other, he faced huge opposition. People laughed at him, told him this was an audacious plan, impossible to execute! But Ratan Tata persisted.

No sane person would have dared to declare this plan to the world or even work on it privately. Ratan Tata was a loner in this journey, but guided by his radical thinking, bizarre philosophies, and bold actions, he made it happen. He brought out the world's cheapest car at INR 1,20,000 (US $3000) a first in the history of the automobile industry.

Though Tata Nano as a project has not been successful, Ratan Tata certainly sparked a worldwide revolution and now following his innovation, hundreds of other players in the automobile industry are attempting similar creations. They will come up with their own versions of the Tata Nano and learning from Ratan Tata's experiences and mistakes, may soon create a model more effective than the Nano as well, but the credit for conceiving this idea shall always remain with Ratan Tata.

In less than two years, he has embarked on the second most ambitious project, 'Tata Megapixel Concept Car' which he unveiled at the Geneva Motor Show. The car runs at an average of 100 kmpl (kilometer per litre). It will use a unique combination of technologies and will be rolled out in three years. A concept which is unheard of and again he is alone on this journey!

Let's shift from the corporate world and step into the political arena for a moment. Aung San Suu Kyi — the internationally acclaimed politician — is a pro-democracy leader of Burma (now Myanmar). She is the daughter of Burma's independence hero Aung San who was assassinated when she was only two years old. After her father's demise, she moved to India with her mother who was then elected as the Burmese Ambassador to India and Nepal. She was educated in Burma, India, and United Kingdom where she met her husband Michael Aris and the two tied the knot in 1972 and became proud parents of two sons shortly after that.

An ordinary Burmese girl that she was till then, extraordinariness was planted in her by her father whom she knew had given up his life for the welfare of his country and countrymen.

She stayed outside Burma throughout her life, but there was something that attached her to her home country and as fate would have it, Aung San Suu Kyi returned to her homeland in 1988 to nurse her dying mother. Enraged by the military junta raj prevalent in Burma, she soon became engaged in the country's nationwide democracy uprising and founded a pro-democracy party called the National League for Democracy in the same year to fight for human rights.

Since 1988 she has left all her individual desires aside, took up the singular cause of the Burmese Republic. Since she started this movement, she has been detained several times, spending more than 15 years in detention, most of it under house arrest, but this did not shake her resolve to fight for her nation. While under house arrest, she spent her time reading philosophy, politics, and biographies that took her closer to her cause and each time she was freed, she would test the limits of the junta's tolerance by campaigning throughout the country, delivering speeches at several occasions, awakening the Burmese population to stand up for democracy.

She was also awarded the most prestigious Nobel Peace Prize in 1991. In 1997, her husband was diagnosed with prostate cancer, which turned out to be terminal. Despite appeals from prominent figures and organisations, including the United States, UN Secretary General Kofi Annan and Pope John Paul II, the Burmese government would not grant him a visa to come and meet his beloved wife one last time. Though Aung San Suu Kyi was offered the chance to go and meet her dying husband, she refused the chance to leave Burma because she could not abandon her people. She knew that once she left Burma she would not be allowed to return, thus separating her from her cause forever. While under house arrest she was also separated from her children, who lived in the United Kingdom, but Suu Kyi did not give up.

She always had the choice to change her path and spend time with her ailing husband and lovely children. But it was acceptable to her to give up on her family attachments, but she could not afford to be detached from her cause. Her cause — democracy for Burma was far more important than the life of her husband, her two sons and herself. And she has always responded to questions about the sacrifices she has made in her personal life by saying these are nothing compared to the suffering of Burma's people.

What did Aung San Suu Kyi have with her through this fight? Whom did she have on her side or supporting her when she stood up against the almighty military raj? Whom did she have next to her when she was put on house arrest for one-quarter of her life? But her spirit and resolve was not once shaken once by these trivial thoughts for she knew that she is a Life Maximizer and Life Maximizers are loners in their journey.

Eighteen years is not a short time. But the life she has chosen to lead has been a beacon of hope for the people of Burma. Even today she is steadfast in her commitment to the nation, but she is still alone. She won't give up, compromise or sink into the crowd around her!

Life Maximizers are loners from within. They may have people around them — relationships that may matter, possessions that they may value, but yet they are loners. Their only attachment is with their cause and in order to remain attached to their cause, they remain detached as human beings. When you are attached to people around you — your family, friends, kids etc., or with things such as your house, office, or car, your mind is preoccupied and this distracts you from life maximization. However, life maximizers, though attached to their family, kids, home, office or car, maintain a sense of detachment from all their attachments.

Life Maximizers work best as loners for being lonely gives them the space, the time and opportunity to think about and get closer to their cause. There is a private conversation that happens between a Life Maximizer and his cause when he/she is alone. There is a certain romance that surfaces, a relationship that develops and it is only this attachment that they nurture throughout life while all other worldly connections remain only as significant as they should, not allowing the Life Maximizer to flow into them and digress from their cause.

Thus, my dear friends, being a 'loner' is not the outcome of being a Life Maximizer or the consequence of being abandoned by people while you work towards Life Maximization, but a very deliberate act of distancing oneself from the world in order to be a Life Maximizer!

In the next one week, make a conscious attempt to think, speak, and act in a manner different from the thoughts, words, and actions of the crowd around you.

My dear friends, if you want to be Life Maximizers you will have to be alone, you will have to be alone, you will have to be alone... period. Understand this, accept this, and be ready for it! Declare it to the whole world. If people endorse your ideas and come along with you, it is a bonus. But don't keep that as a condition. As I said, the world is full of people from the crowd. They will only join you when you have been proved right, because the crowd wants proof, endorsements, and a guarantee.

A Life Maximizer will never bother about all this. He is never afraid of threats or death. He will die for his idea, but cannot be put to death by the crowd.

When in the 16th century, Galileo declared that the earth revolved around the sun and not the other way round, he was ridiculed, tortured and even threatened to make him withdraw his statements. However, he had the courage to challenge the establishment although he was alone. Today, hundreds of years after that, we all know that he was right; science has proved it and every child on earth knows this fact.

The beauty of a Life Maximizer is that he challenges the crowd and keeps doing that for a long time. When he/she feels it is difficult, impossible to hold fort, he pretends to be a member of the crowd. But the truth is that he is pretending, buying time. He will sit in the crowd and work out a new strategy to come back powerfully. History has always proved it. It happened in the case of Galileo and it will keep happening, for Life Maximizers never give up and they never look back. They don't ever have the time for regrets!

From the examples of all these great men and women — be it Ratan Tata, Aung San Suu Kyi, Galileo or the others mentioned in this book — I learned that if you want to maximize life, you have to decide whether you want to be a part of the crowd or be the odd man out and I declared to be a loner.

In order to maximize life for a lifetime, you need to give this order, this instruction, this directive, this mandate, this law of God, this commandment every day, every hour, every minute of your life:

Be ready to be a loner.

COMMANDMENT

10

Declare that you will be 'Forever Alive'

You can only be 'Forever Alive' if you have something significant yet to do in life.

Life maximization is a long lonely process of continuously expiring your current self, thinking beyond possibilities and distancing yourself from emotionally draining distractions by single handedly maximizing all resources around you and rocking the boat of life in the middle of the sea such that you live a life which is:

- **Autonomous**
- **Forever Alive**
- **Led by strong thoughts, words, and deeds**
- **That of a Leader**
- **Difficult to be Duplicated**

Thereby maximizing life for a lifetime.

I would request you to read the above definition, a minimum of five times right now before you proceed.

This is an endless game, and to remain relevant in this game, you have to declare your intention about health, because without good health you cannot do 1% of what a Life Maximizer does in a lifetime.

According to me there is life and then there is death, i.e. you are born on 29 September, 1964 and you will die on the 29 September, 2084. Birth is guaranteed, death is guaranteed. You will go through childhood, teen age, adulthood, middle age, old age... but that does not make any difference. Life has to be lived as a single piece between birth and death.

Don't live life in stages. Life is a single piece — one piece for 120 years. Live it like that.

I have not said that I will be a Life Maximizer till 35, or 47, 59 or 89. I will be a Life Maximizer till I die! And in order to maximize life, you too will have to take this pledge, because life maximization only ends with death.

- Dev Anand, a great Indian actor and director died at 88, few months after the release of his last film.
- Kishore Kumar, a great Indian singer, lived till 58.
- M.F. Hussain, a great Indian painter, left this world when he was 95, having earned the reputation of being one of the greatest Indian painters of all times.
- J.R.D Tata, a great Indian industrialist departed at 89.
- Peter Drucker, the great management guru lived till 95 and was writing till his last days.
- Queen Elizabeth is still going strong at 86.
- Pandit Ravishankar, a great sitar player, was still creating music till he passed away at 92.
- Zohra Sehgal, a great actress, is alive and kicking at 100.
- Asha Bhonsale, a celebrated Indian singing icon, is mesmerising people with her songs at 79.
- A.P.J Abdul Kalam, former president of India is still inspiring and motivating at 80.
- The 14th Dalai Lama, is full of life at 76.
- Richard Branson, a great British Entrepreneur, raring to go at 61.
- Martina Navratilova, a great tennis player playing at the age of 55.

→ Hema Malini and Rekha — two iconic Indian actresses, vibrant and zestful at 63 and 57 respectively.

The beauty of these individuals is that they did not die before they died. Those alive are alive... that is the meaning of being Forever Alive!

You don't get to choose how and when you are going to die; you can only choose how you are going to live.

~ Joan Baez

I asked myself one day, 'How long do I plan to live?' No one asks such a question because some people think it is unlucky, it is embarrassing, 'it is not in my hands'. Some don't ask this question believing that they will not die at all.

I still believe each one of us has an age in mind. So don't worry, kill your fear and ask yourself, 'How long do you plan to live?' Ask this question and write down an age that comes to your mind in this block:

I will live till:______

When I asked this question many, many years ago, I said to myself,

I will live till 95

Now ask yourself another question, 'How will your life be one year before you die?' Imagine your:

- Body
- Psychology
- Wealth
- Relationships
- What will you be doing that year?

When I asked myself, how I will be at 94, the answers that I got were:

Body — No illness, in top condition, travelling

Psychology — Very alert, powerful, upgrading myself, taking on challenges

Wealth — Giving away INR 10 crore every year to charity

Relationships — Powerful and bonded, connecting with all my friends, family and the whole world

What I will be doing that year:

- Writing bestsellers
- Making new audios, videos on new subjects (or whichever formats are popular then)
- Travelling to educate the world
- Inspiring and motivating millions around the world
- Creating value by being a leader and giving direction to people

- Relating with a whole new bunch of people and giving them confidence
- Manufacturing new, creative ideas and making people more capable

I will never say:

- Now I am 50 or 60
- I am so old
- I have fulfilled all my worldly responsibilities
- I have done the best I can
- I am just waiting to go away from this world
- I am waiting for God's call

People who say this lose their enthusiasm, persistence, accountability, commitment, purpose, money, friends, and all relationships.

If you believe that you are old or are getting old and you cannot grow or contribute anymore, nature starts taking away most of your healthy body parts, you actually start getting old and become worthless to yourself and everyone around you. And the moment you become worthless to yourself and the world around you, the world starts ignoring you, including your near and dear ones.

Life Maximizers have understood that the world values you only till the day you are beneficial to people around you and if you are contributing to the ecosystem for its progress. Therefore, they decide to be forever alive.

Each of the people mentioned in this book have been significant contributors to the world till the last day of their life. Those alive are contributing even to this day and shall remain contributors as long as they exist.

Life Maximizers are alive in their spirit.

How are Life Maximizers alive in spirit?

1. They see things differently
2. They feel differently about the future
3. They think differently about the future
4. They communicate differently about the future
5. They act differently for the future

1. Seeing things differently

- ► They see the future as an endless ocean
- ► They see themselves around for 100-150 years

2. Feeling differently about the future

- ► They can maintain their youth and vibrancy forever

3. Thinking differently about the future

- ► They think beyond themselves
- ► They can make a difference to the world till they live and even after they die

4. Communicating differently about the future

- ► They communicate with passion in a manner that people are compelled to act

5. **Acting differently for the future**

   - ► They act swiftly and take on newer projects
   - ► They are unafraid of taking risks and unafraid of losing
   - ► They act like there is no one stopping them
   - ► They act with the belief that they can:
     - Change the world
     - Heal the world
     - Make the world a better place
     - Impact the world
   - ► Get the support needed from the universe to accomplish their dreams.

They take the future in their hands and behave as if the future is their property. Their belief in ageless living and endless energy comes from the following three attitudes:

1. **No-Age Attitude:** Life Maximizers are not particularly bothered with what age they are for they believe there is no age at which one starts or stops maximizing life. How else would you define the life of Col. Sanders who started the famous fast food chain called KFC (Kentucky Fried Chicken) at 79 — an age at which ordinary mortals are probably on pilgrimage tours if not already bedridden.

2. **No-Retirement Attitude:** Life Maximizers never retire. They may retire from their jobs/businesses at a certain age but this state of retirement does not come in way of life maximization. E. Shreedharan, a railway engineer took the challenge of building the Delhi Metro, years after his retirement, and

became the Managing Director of the Delhi Metro Project at 70+. Back then, he knew head nor tail about the setting up of a metro railway system. But he went ahead and learnt the rules of this new game that he had ventured into and was so successful that people called him the 'Metro Man'. At 80, he is a consultant to various state governments.

3. **Lifetime Usefulness:** Life Maximizers have the urge to remain useful and contribute to the world as long as their heart beats. At 88, when Brij Mohan Munjal could have just continued to thrive on the success of Hero Honda, he decided to amicably end his 26-year-old partnership with Honda and took the plunge of establishing himself as Hero MotoCorp, independently producing two-wheelers in India thus embodying the philosophy of lifetime usefulness, and being forever alive.

Above all, Life Maximizers challenge the Law of Diminishing Returns. They grow older only in age. They don't believe that they will contribute any less as their age progresses. On the contrary, they believe the opposite, i.e. their returns to the world every year will be more than what they gave the previous year.

Now let's come back to my questions. Sometime back I asked you, 'How long do you plan to live?' You must have given an age, like I gave 95 years.

Then I asked you another interesting question, 'How will your life be one year before you die?', i.e. how would your body, psychology, wealth, relationships be, and what would you be doing that year? I am sure you have your answers ready now.

My third question now is, ***If you live life in this positive and progressive manner, do you think you will die at your planned age?***

The obvious answer is NO.

My fourth question is, ***How long will you live if you do not die at your planned age?***

When I asked this question to myself some years ago, I said to myself, ***I will live till 120.***

I call these 25 special 'bonus' years as ***Journey Extension.***

In Mumbai (where I reside), when you have a monthly railway pass from Destination A to Destination B and you wish to go a little further to Destination C, you can take a 'Journey Extension' from B to C. So with 25 more years as my Journey Extension, I will live till 120.

My fifth and last question, ***What would Santosh Nair do in these 25 'bonus' years?***

And my answer was:

- Win the Nobel Prize
- Become the most powerful voice in this world
- Create 1500 audio, videos instead of the 1000 that I was to create by 95
- Write 150 books instead of the 100 that I was to write till 95
- Make **smm**art the world's largest individual, entrepreneur and enterprise transformation company
- Achieve all the goals I have written for Q5 in Chapter 7 (What would I like to do before I leave this world?)

Living life in the manner described above is known as being forever alive. But amidst all the daily complexities of life, this picture gets forgotten too soon. Hence, you need to be reminded of your goals from time-to-time and this cannot be done by yourself or by appointing an assistant who will remind you, or by the use of technology. You will have to create a group of people who are with you in this philosophy and that's where we come to the most important concept — **Journey Extension Buddy Group.**

A Journey Extension Buddy Group is a group of people who are like you — healthy, forever alive, living life until they die. These people have also declared their intention to maximize life like you and being in their company will only take you closer to your goal of being forever alive. For one reason or the other, the Buddy Group may keep getting smaller, but as the self-proclaimed leader of the Buddy Group, you will have to ensure that the buddy group keeps on expanding. If any member leaves, three new members have to be added and the enthusiasm and youthfulness of the group has to be kept alive.

List four people who can be a part of your Journey Extension Buddy Group and describe how you will interact with them and be forever alive.

Ageing is a concept of the twentieth century. It is a self-fulfilling prophecy. You often tend to become what you think. If you think you are old, you are old; if you think you will be forever alive, you will be forever alive. Through your thoughts, communication, and actions, show people that you will live life king-size, beyond 100. Let everybody around you see it, feel it, believe it, and love it. Predict and create your great future. Live your great future! Maximize time, resources, opportunities… maximize life!

In order to maximize life for a lifetime, you need to give this order, this instruction, this directive, this mandate, this law of God, this commandment every day, every hour, every minute of your life:

Declare that you will be 'Forever Alive'.

11

Live a life that is difficult to duplicate

If your life is easily duplicable, you are not a Life Maximizer.

We have come to the last chapter, my dear friends, the last commandment of these set of eleven that I have learnt in life and used to maximize myself and those around me and this one is nothing but a culmination of the previous 10, I would say!

I spoke about the difference between 'living life and spending it' in the very first chapter of this book. I don't know if I was in a position to successfully communicate back then what it meant, but if I wasn't, let's look at it once again.

Most people spend their life consuming things, but those Life Maximizers as we now know them, are creators. Creators don't consume and consumers don't create.

Creators create corporations, institutions, nations, and monuments. The consumers, on the other hand — the ordinary mortals — work for these corporations or institutions; be a part of the creation of these nations or monuments and consume products and services produced by the creators.

Those who are Life Maximizers make a very conscious decision, very early in their life — they decide to be creators, not consumers and so they live a life that cannot be easily duplicated.

And for a man to be a creator, he need not be on this planet for a long period of time. His life can be as short as anybody else's and yet he can do in this one lifetime what is difficult to be duplicated by another human being over centuries.

Let's look at Apple — an innovation madness company. Behind Apple was a man called Steve Jobs whose visit to this planet was only for 56 years and in this short period, he transformed four industries. It is difficult to change one industry in a lifetime and he did it to four — the music industry with iTunes; the movie industry with Pixar; the computer industry with iPad/Mac; the telecommunications industry with iPhone... and the quest for the next gamechanger continued till the end of his life.

A college dropout, Steve Jobs co-founded Apple in 1976 with a friend Steve Wozniak (called Woz) and set it up in Steve's family garage. Along with Woz, Steve put his heart and soul into building Apple — his first love and within 10 years, it had grown into a $2 billion company with over 4000 employees. Steve was 30 by then. In due course, they hired a man who Steve thought was fit to run the company along with him but after their very first year, their visions of the future were not the same, they had a falling out. The Board of Directors supported the other man and Steve was fired.

He was dethroned in his own company and what had been the singular focus of his entire adult life was shattered in a few moments. But Steve did not give up on life. He started two new ventures — Pixar Studios that created the world's first computer animated feature film *Toy Story* and many others before it merged with Walt Disney in 2006, making Steve Jobs Disney's largest shareholder; the second was a computer hardware and software company called NeXT which, in another turn of events, was bought over by Apple thus bringing Steve back to his first love as its CEO once again.

In his second innings at Apple, he launched marvelous products and at startling speeds — difficult to duplicate!

Almost immediately after Apple released a new product, competitors would scramble to produce comparable technologies, but never were they successful at taking the lead. Steve introduced revolutionary products such as the MacBook Air, iPod, and iPhone, all of which have dictated the evolution of modern technology and the impact is so high that 2 million pieces of his iPhone 5 sold out on the day of its launch. Phew… is that really possible!

'If you live each day as if it was your last, someday you'll most certainly be right.' He came across this quote as a 17-year-old and it became the very foundation of his life. He lived each day as if it was his last day and worked till the last day of his life for he enjoyed his work and loved it more than anything else in the world. When he was diagnosed with pancreatic cancer for many years he kept conquering the pain, sacrificed all the pleasures in his life, and lived for a cause bigger than himself.

What differentiated Steve Jobs from ordinary mortals were two of his fundamentals qualities:

1. Unreasonableness
2. Impracticality

Impracticality is defined by T.T. Rangarajan, one of my great friends and an Indian spiritual coach as:

Impracticality is the vocabulary of a mediocre person who does not want to take responsibility of implementation.

Steve Jobs was an impractical fanatic in love with his work. He took complete responsibility for the creations he believed in; he took responsibility for the implementation of his vision and converted what ordinary folks thought an impractical dream into practical reality. Apple, the world's most valuable company today has a market value of $656 billion.

The quality, not the longevity of one's life is important.
~ Martin Luther King Jr

Going by Martin Luther King Jr.'s words, Steve Jobs lived a quality life, if not a long one. And in the process, he conquered physical, mental, and psychological pain. He conquered emotions, he conquered day and night. He did that extra bit and made ordinary situations extraordinary. He worked extra, travelled extra, spoke extra, read extra, built extra, and developed extra capabilities and skills. He had a lot of passion, determination, dedication, sincerity, discipline, and excitement and became an extraordinary individual — a Life Maximizer! His life is difficult to duplicate and that is the last commandment you have to give yourself. Remember to consciously and proactively work towards it!

In order to maximize life for a lifetime, you need to give this order, this instruction, this directive, this mandate, this law of God, this commandment every day, every hour, every minute of your life:

Live a life that is difficult to duplicate.

Epilogue

We have come to the end of this book, my dear friends. What I shared through the eleven chapters were not theoretical philosophies, but the very essence of my life. Each commandment I have presented has been the guiding principle of my life. They constitute the foundation of all that I have achieved and the rest of my life's goals are within my reach because I believe in them, and all that I have shared with you in this conversation.

Few, if not all, of the commandments would have certainly intrigued you, forced you to look at life in a different way. Some of them you might have already started practising, or shortly will as you encounter life more closely in the days to come. But before you do that I would request you to go back to the beginning of this book and revisit all the eleven commandments that you have read so far, and I said read — not internalized.

The essence of Life Maximization lies in the totality of this book — all the eleven commandments and not one/two/five of them. You will never be able to maximize life by following a select few of these philosophies as the magic is created by the power of the eleven together since they are all intertwined and interconnected. And when you follow each of these commandments, accept them, imbibe them in your psyche and internalize them in a manner that you become a living demonstration of these commandments, you would have maximized life.

Your life will be the epitome of wisdom, possibility thinking, the epitome of rocking the boat in the middle of the sea, of autonomy, as well as the epitome of maximizing resources, the epitome of positivity in your thoughts, words, and deeds, certainly the epitome of leadership, of distancing yourself from emotionally draining distractions, of loneliness, and finally the epitome of living a non-duplicable life. You will live a life that will take an ordinary man 40 lifetimes to replicate and that is the true pinnacle of Life Maximization!

When I look back at all these eleven commandments together, there is one man who embodies all of them, whose history we studied in the eleventh chapter. He has lived not only the eleventh commandment, but all the eleven commandments of Life Maximization and is a pure representation of each one of them. Steve Jobs!

In conclusion I would like to pay tribute to this innovation genius who embodies the very essence of Life Maximization, who personifies each one of the eleven commandments that we have learnt so far and let's take a look at how he did that:

- ➜ Steve was never satisfied with what he was doing and where he was. He constantly expired his current self and kept innovating products that nobody even dreamt of. He was the greatest innovator second only to the legendary Thomas Edison.
- ➜ He was a possibility thinker. He started Apple from his father's garage and made it a multi-billion dollar company.
- ➜ He rocked the boat in the middle of the sea. While leading a successful venture in the computer industry, he ventured into the telecommunications, movie, and music industry unafraid of how this would impact his present glory and success and yet he emerged victorious in all his endeavours.

- ➔ He was an autonomous individual. He dropped out of college as soon as he realised there was no value in it and instead decided to focus on things that would make him what he is today. He lived by the laws he imposed on himself and created the world's most valuable company out of absolutely nothing.
- ➔ He maximized every resource around him and created an institution that employs over 60,000 employees.
- ➔ He was always positive and inspiring in his thoughts, words, and deeds. He was thrown out of his own company, but he was not shattered. He set himself up to create something even bigger and better than what he had done before.
- ➔ He remained a leader throughout his life and kept striving for his cause, which was pure innovation, innovation, innovation!
- ➔ He distanced himself from emotionally draining distractions. He was the son of an unmarried couple who put him up for adoption immediately as he was born. He found out about this when he was in his mid-twenties and met his biological parents too, but never allowed this truth to emotionally break him down.
- ➔ He was a loner in life. He was known for radical thinking, bizarre philosophies, and bold actions and remained detached from the whole world while his only attachment was with his cause — Apple Inc.
- ➔ He was forever alive. Although pancreatic cancer was unbeatable, he did not give up on life. He fought this terminal illness in such a beautiful manner that he lived life until he died, working till his last day.
- ➔ He lived a life that is difficult to be duplicated. In his short

lifetime he transformed four industries and created the world's most miraculous company that will remain alive many years after his death.

How many lives will it take for an ordinary human being to create another Apple?

I suspect it will take 40 lifetimes.

Can the life of Steve Jobs be duplicated?

It is difficult.

He made a difference to this world and the world will remember him forever.

Can you think of a life like that?

Are you ready to risk your present comfort to reach there?

Are you ready to start all over again if this fails?

Are you ready to give it a shot?

Can you visualise that life?

Can you even attempt it?

If the answer to the above questions is 'yes', your visit to this planet is worthwhile and contributory; if not, you can die any moment from now for your life is not worth living!

All the best. Happy Life Maximization!

References

- Ackoff, R. L., 'From Data to Wisdom', Journal of Applies Systems Analysis, Volume 16, 1989 pp 3-9
- 'Information, Preferences and Knowledge, An Interesting Evolution in Thought' by Adam Maria Gadomski
- 'The Origin of the Data Information Knowledge Wisdom Hierarchy' by Nikhil Sharma,
- wikipedia.org
- http://www.thecolorsofindia.com/dadasaheb-phalke/father-indian-cinema.html
- 'The Power of Vision' by Joel Barker
- 'The Business of Paradigms' by Joel Barker
- 'The Miracle Man' – Morris Goodman
- *The Economic Times* articles
- http://www.vridhamma.org/Meditation-Camp-in-Tihar-Jail
- http://business.mapsofindia.com/business-leaders/dhirubhai-ambani.html
- http://www.communityofchrist.net/Potpourri/10_Paradoxical_Commandments/10_paradoxical_commandments.html
- Webster's Dictionary & Oxford Dictionary
- http://www.nobelprize.org/nobel_prizes/chemistry/laureates/1911/marie-curie-bio.html

- http://www.spartacus.schoolnet.co.uk/USAford.htm
- http://grasshopper.com/blog/2011/11/the-early-failures-of-famous-entrepreneurs-and-what-they-learned-3/
- http://beyondbelief2010.wordpress.com/2011/01/25/failures-of-bill-gates-henry-ford-and-other-famous-entrepreneurs/
- http://www.des.emory.edu/mfp/efficacynotgiveup.html
- http://www.mouseplanet.com/9365/Of_Failure_and_Success_The_Journey_of_Walt_Disney
- http://www.entrepreneur.com/slideshow/219445
- http://www.progress.org/gandhi/gandhi03.htm
- http://bornpowerful.com/2010/11/mother-teresa-her-heroic-heart-inspired-many/
- http://www.afternoondc.in/sports/mother-told-me-to-play-for-the-country-after-fathers-death-tendulkar/article_17098
- http://www.indianexpress.com/news/father-dead-he-bats-to-save-delhi/18988/
- http://articles.timesofindia.indiatimes.com/2008-03-03/top-stories/27755869_1_virat-kohli-ranji-criminal-lawyer
- http://www.theweekendleader.com/Success/1298/Change-within.html
- http://www.womensweb.in/articles/inspiring-woman-anu-aga/
- http://www.burmacampaign.org.uk/index.php/burma/about-burma/about-burma/a-biography-of-aung-san-suu-kyi
- http://www.ted.com/talks/steve_jobs_how_to_live_before_you_die.html
- http://www.biography.com/people/steve-jobs-9354805
- http://articles.businessinsider.com/2011-10-06/tech/30249828_1_college-tuition-calligraphy-adoption

About smmart

smmart Training & Consultancy Services Pvt. Ltd is the brainchild of Santosh Nair and one of India's finest entrepreneur transformation companies.

Having started off as a Corporate Training Company, **smm**art has in the last 13 years spread its wings to encompass various industries and forms of training, including motivational pep talks, classroom training programmes, outbound training, interactive/ activity-based workshops, entrepreneurial training, and so on.

smmart's expertise lies in:

1. Motivational programmes
2. Sales training programmes, short and long-term with periodic reviews
3. Negotiation
4. Leadership Development
5. Key Account Management
6. Any other skill and attitudinal programme customised to the requirement of an organisation
7. CEO Coaching and Mentoring
8. Entrepreneurial development by conducting short and long term programmes with periodic reviews

9. Personal coaching, consulting and enablement for small and mid-sized entrepreneurs

10. Institutionalizing systems and processes and the overall development of small and mid-sized organisations etc.

Some of the finest corporations trained by **smm**art are:

1. Aptech Ltd.
2. Asian Paints (India) Ltd.
3. Aviva Life Insurance
4. Axis Bank Ltd
5. Bajaj Allianz
6. Bharati AXA
7. Bharati Cellular Ltd. (Airtel)
8. Birla Mutual Funds
9. Birla Sun Life Insurance
10. Coca Cola
11. DLF Ltd.
12. Dun & Bradstreet
13. Ford Motors
14. Hindustan Unilever
15. HDFC Standard Life
16. HSBC Bank
17. Hyundai Motors
18. ICICI Bank
19. IDEA CELLULAR
20. Ion Exchange
21. ITW India Ltd.
22. John Deere
23. Kotak Life Insurance
24. Mahindra & Mahindra
25. Max Life Insurance Co. Ltd.
26. MetLife
27. New Holland Tractors
28. Om Kotak Mahindra
29. Philips
30. Proctor & Gamble
31. Reliance Life Insurance
32. Saint Gobain Glass

33. Sodexo
34. Standard Chartered Bank
35. State Bank of India
36. SBI Life Insurance
37. SKF Bearings
38. Tata - AIG
39. Tata Sky Ltd.
40. Tata VSNL
41. Vodafone Essar Ltd.
42. Several other small and mid-sized enterprises

To know more about our training programmes or to engage our services to transform yourself and your organisation, you can contact us at:

smmart Training & Consultancy Services Pvt. Ltd.
506, Akruti Arcade
Opp. Wadia School, J.P. Road,
Andheri (West),
Mumbai 400 053
India.
Ph: 022 6772 9000
www.smmart.co.in

Santosh Nair's Knowledge Products & Merchandise Pvt. Ltd.

Santosh Nair's Knowledge Products & Merchandise Pvt. Ltd. is Santosh Nair's endeavour to inspire excellence and transformation. This initiative deals with knowledge products and merchandise.

The brand that is 'Santosh Nair' represents a powerful knowledge bank and the audios, videos, books, and merchandise such as calendars, mugs, t-shirts with Santosh Nair's quotes, are available across the country.

Each of these knowledge products and merchandise acts as a thunderbolt, inspiring people to rebel against themselves by awakening them to their present realities and helping them unleash their true potential.

Some of the bestselling audios and videos brought out by Santosh Nair are:

Confidence Multiplier: 'Confidence is the Eternal Ability to remain composed, alert and directed in all our thoughts, words, and deeds when faced with the Fears and Insecurities that surround us.' In this four-hour self-empowering programme, Santosh Nair delivers an inspiring speech about the meaning and importance of confidence; the five things that confident people do and the three essential qualities of confident individuals thus enabling viewers to protect and multiply their confidence.

Future Multiplier: Our future is our own property and we need to take care of it well to reap maximum benefits from it over time. In this four-hour programme, Santosh Nair talks about the University of Life and the 12 goals one needs to set and achieve to multiply one's future.

Success Multiplier: Success doesn't come naturally to many people. There are certain predetermined formulas that have to be understood and practised in order to be successful in life. In this four-hour pep talk, Santosh Nair enlightens the audience about how one can become successful in every aspect of life and also unveils the six formulas for success!

Eleven Commandments of Life Maximization: The inspiration for this book in your hands, this CD explains the eleven directives, mandates, demands, instructions, or the 'Laws of God', fondly called 'The Eleven Commandments of Life Maximization' that one needs to follow to maximize every day, every hour, every minute, and every moment of your life. A must watch especially after you've read the book!

Productivity Multiplier: This is an insightful and interactive programme, which will ensure that you are productive, confident, and happy even through the most frustrating and challenging situations in life. It will teach you to identify and use these tools productively, through the most advanced techniques of ABCDE and Rational Emotive Behavior Therapy so you can substitute every negative emotion and belief with a positive one.

Sales Multiplier: All human beings have to sell something in life; be it an entrepreneur, a salesperson, a teacher, a child, a parent, a boss, or a subordinate. In this power-packed CD, Santosh Nair, the legend in sales, enlightens the audience about the innovative techniques of reducing time, increasing momentum, and bringing about a meaningful transformation while selling an idea, a product, or a thought, thus making life easier, vibrant, progressive and successful.

Opportunity Multiplier: In this four-hour life transforming revelation, Santosh Nair talks about the two diseases that most of us are suffering from: 100% Accuracy Syndrome (Jo Bhi Karunga, Perfect Karunga) and Chronic Tomorrow Syndrome (Jo Bhi Karunga, Kal Se Karunga). The only antidote to this disease is The smmart 75% Opportunity Mantra that will show you how you can grab all opportunities to multiply your business, health, wealth, relationships, capabilities, and life.

Trust Multiplier: The one thing that is required for success is trust. If nurtured well, it can lead to great prosperity and if lost, it can destroy successful corporations, or relationships forever. Trust Multiplier gives you easy to adopt techniques and 15 Attributes to permanently become a DTR in life: Dependable, Trustworthy, and Reliable.

Leadership Multiplier: In this fiery programme, Santosh Nair offers enlightenment about:

- Who is a leader?
- How are leaders manufactured?
- Characteristics of a leader
- Five Levels of Leadership
- 14 Predominant Leadership Lessons

Change Multiplier: The world around us is changing. People are changing, relationships are changing, industries are changing, economies are changing, situations and circumstances in which people operated earlier, are all changing! To match pace with these changing times and to remain relevant and at par with the world, you have to build a DNA of change and become a Change Multiplier. Learn the art of

Change Multiplication from Santosh Nair. Understand the Eight-Point Gameplan for leading change in organisations.

Distinct Forte Multiplier: You should only do what you love to do. And if you do this for ten years or 10,000 hours, you will become a genius in your field. In this life transforming revelation, Santosh Nair explains:

- What does Distinct Forte mean?
- D.F.F. i.e. Distinct Forte Fears that keep you away from your Distinct Forte
- Distinct Forte Five Power Process: Identifying your Distinct Forte
- Distinct Forte Squad: Your support team for your Distinct Forte

Responsibility Multiplier: Responsibility evasion is a committed way of life. It is a neurosis; a psychosis; a state of drunken bliss, so deeply ingrained in your philosophies that the fact that you're evading responsibility does not even occur to you; ultimately blocking your own progress and of those around you. In this programme, Santosh Nair differentiates between a Responsibility Evader and a Responsibility Multiplier, highlighting the 11 Characteristics of a Responsibility Evader and the six formulas to make you a Responsibility Multiplier.

Winning in Uncertain Times: Currently, we are all facing uncertain times. This period can be defined as a period of personal and professional turmoil: a time of confusion, paranoia, hopelessness, anxiety, depression, pain, and stress. In this four-hour power-packed programme, Santosh Nair talks about winning and the eight formulas that are required to be a winner despite uncertain times.

Why do Entrepreneurs Miss the Bus:

- Do you think you are a successful entrepreneur?
- Is your business growing year-on-year?
- Are you taking your organisation to the next level?
- Do you enjoy being an entrepreneur?

Whether your answer to these questions is 'yes' or 'no', this programme shall be a eye-opener, take you on the path of entrepreneurial excellence, helping you enjoy entrepreneurship with every passing moment.